English Men of Letters

EDITED BY JOHN MORLEY

SOUTHEY

SOUTHEY

BY

EDWARD DOWDEN

AMS PRESS
NEW YORK

Reprinted from the edition of 1888, London
First AMS EDITION published 1968
Manufactured in the United States of America

Library of Congress Catalogue Card Number: 68-58377

74868

AMS PRESS, INC.
New York, N.Y. 10003

NOTE.

I AM indebted throughout to *The Life and Correspondence of Robert Southey,* edited by the Rev. C. C. Southey, six volumes, 1850, and to *Selections from the Letters of Robert Southey,* edited by J. W. Warter, B.D., four volumes, 1856. Many other sources have been consulted. I thank Mr. W. J. Craig for help given in examining Southey manuscripts, and Mr. T. W. Lyster for many valuable suggestions.

CONTENTS.

SOUTHEY.

CHAPTER I.

CHILDHOOD.

No one of his generation lived so completely in and for
literature as did Southey. " He is," said Byron, " the only
existing entire man of letters." With him literature
served the needs both of the material life and of the life
of the intellect and imagination; it was his means of
earning daily bread, and also the means of satisfying his
highest ambitions and desires. This which was true of
Southey at five-and-twenty years of age was equally true
at forty, fifty, sixty. During all that time he was actively
at work accumulating, arranging, and distributing knowledge ; no one among his contemporaries gathered so large
a store from the records of the past ; no one toiled with
such steadfast devotion to enrich his age ; no one occupied
so honourable a place in so many provinces of literature.
There is not perhaps any single work of Southey's the
loss of which would be felt by us as a capital misfortune.
But the more we consider his total work, its mass, its
variety, its high excellence, the more we come to regard
it as a memorable, an extraordinary achievement.

Southey himself, however, stands above his works. In subject they are disconnected, and some of them appear like huge fragments. It is the presence of one mind, one character in all, easily recognizable by him who knows Southey, which gives them a vital unity. We could lose the *History of Brazil*, or the *Peninsular War*, or the *Life of Wesley*, and feel that if our possessions were diminished, we ourselves in our inmost being had undergone no loss which might not easily be endured. But he who has once come to know Southey's voice as the voice of a friend, so clear, so brave, so honest, so full of boyish glee, so full of manly tenderness, feels that if he heard that voice no more a portion of his life were gone. To make acquaintance with the man is better than to study the subjects of his books. In such a memoir as the present, to glance over the contents of a hundred volumes, dealing with matters widely remote, would be to wander upon a vast circumference when we ought to strike for the centre. If the reader come to know Southey as he read and wrote in his library, as he rejoiced and sorrowed among his children, as he held hands with good old friends, as he walked by the lakeside, or lingered to muse near some mountain stream, as he hoped and feared for England, as he thought of life and death and a future beyond the grave, the end of this small book will have been attained.

At the age of forty-six Robert Southey wrote the first of a series of autobiographic sketches ; his spirit was courageous, and life had been good to him ; but it needed more than his courage to live again in remembrance with so many of the dead ; having told the story of his boy-hood, he had not the heart to go farther. The autobio-graphy rambles pleasantly into by-ways of old Bath and Bristol life ; at Westminster School it leaves him. So far

we shall go along with it; for what lies beyond, a record
of Southey's career must be brought together from a mul-
titude of letters, published or still remaining in manuscript,
and from many and massy volumes in prose and verse,
which show how the industrious hours sped by.

Southey's father was a linen-draper of Bristol. He had
left his native fields under the Quantock hills to take
service in a London shop, but his heart suffered in its
exile. The tears were in his eyes one day when a porter
went by carrying a hare, and the remembrance suddenly
came to him of his rural sports. On his master's death
he took a place behind the counter of Britton's shop in
Wine Street, Bristol, and when twelve years later he
opened a shop for himself in the same business he had,
with tender reminiscence, a hare painted for a device
upon his windows. He kept his grandfather's sword
which had been borne in Monmouth's rebellion; he loved
the chimes and quarter-boys of Christ Church, Bristol,
and tried as churchwarden to preserve them. What else
of poetry there may have been in the life of Robert
Southey the elder is lost among the buried epics of pro-
saic lives. We cannot suppose that as a man of business
he was sharp and shrewd; he certainly was not successful.
When the draper's work was done, he whiled away the
hours over Felix Farley's Bristol Journal, his only reading. For library some score of books shared with his
wine-glasses the small cupboard in the back parlour; its
chief treasures were the *Spectator*, the *Guardian*, some
eighteenth-century poems, dead even then, and one or two
immortal plays.

On Sundays Mr. Southey, then a bachelor, would stroll
to Bedminster to dine at the pleasant house of Mrs.
Hill—a substantial house to which Edward Hill, gentle-

man, brought his second wife, herself a widow; a house rich in old English comfort, with its diamond-tiled garden-way and jessamine-covered porch, its wainscoted "best kitchen," its blue room and green room and yellow room, its grapes and green-gages and nectarines, its sweet-williams and stocks and syringas. Among these pleasant surroundings the young draper found it natural on Sabbath afternoons to make love to pleasant Margaret Hill. "Never," writes her son Robert Southey, "never was any human being blessed with a sweeter temper or a happier disposition." Her face had been marred by the seams of small-pox, but its brightness and kindness remained; there was a charm in her clear hazel eyes, so good a temper and so alert an understanding were to be read in them. She had not gone to any school except one for dancing, and "her state," declares Southey, "was the more gracious;" her father had, however, given her lessons in the art of whistling; she could turn a tune like a blackbird. From a mother, able to see a fact swiftly and surely, and who knew both to whistle and to dance, Southey inherited that alertness of intellect and that joyous temper, without which he could not have accomplished his huge task-work, never yielding to a mood of rebellion or *ennui*.

After the courtship on Sunday afternoons came the wedding, and before long a beautiful boy was born, who died in infancy. On the 12th of August, 1774, Mrs. Southey was again in the pain of childbirth. "Is it a boy?" she asked the nurse. "Ay, a great ugly boy!" With such salutation from his earliest critic the future poet-laureate entered this world. "God forgive me," his mother exclaimed afterwards in relating the event, "when I saw what a great red creature it was, covered with rolls of fat, I thought I should never be able to love him."

In due time the red creature proved to be a distinctively
human child whose curly hair and sensitive feelings made
him a mother's darling.   He had not yet heard of sentiment or of Rousseau, but he wept at the pathos of romantic
literature, at the tragic fate of the " Children sliding on
the ice all on a summer's day," or the too early
death of " Billy Pringle's pig," and he would beg the
reciters not to proceed.   His mother's household cares
multiplied, and Southey, an unbreeched boy of three
years, was borne away one morning by his faithful foster-
mother Patty to be handed over to the tender mercies of
a schoolmistress.   Ma'am Powell was old and grim, and
with her lashless eyes gorgonized the new pupil ; on the
seizure of her hand he woke to rebellion, kicking lustily
and crying, "Take me to Pat ! I don't like ye ! you've
got ugly eyes ! take me to Pat, I say ! "   But soft-hearted
Pat had gone home, sobbing.

Mrs. Southey's one weakness was that of submitting
too meekly to the tyranny of an imperious half-sister,
Miss Tyler, the daughter of Grandmother Hill by her first
marriage.   For this weakness there were excuses ; Miss
Tyler was an elder sister by many years ; she had property of her own ; she passed for a person of fashion, and
was still held to be a beauty ; above all, she had the advantage of a temper so capricious and violent that to
quarrel with her at all might be to lose her sisterly regard
for ever.   Her struggling sister's eldest son took Aunt
Tyler's fancy ; it was a part of her imperious kindness to adopt or half-adopt the boy.   Aunt Tyler lived
in Bath ; in no other city could a gentlewoman better
preserve health and good looks, or enjoy so much society
of distinction on easy but not too ample means ; it possessed a charming theatre, and Miss Tyler was a patron

of the drama. To Bath, then, she had brought her portrait by Gainsborough, her inlaid cabinet of ebony, her
cherry-wood arm-chair, her mezzotints after Angelica Kauf-
mann, her old-maid hoards of this and of that, the woman
servant she had saved from the toils of matrimony,
and the old man harmless as one of the crickets which
he nightly fed until he died. To Bath Miss Tyler
also brought her nephew, and she purchased a copy
of the new gospel of education, Rousseau's *Emilius*, in
order to ascertain how Nature should have her perfect
work with a boy in petticoats. Here the little victim,
without companions, without play, without the child's
beatitudes of dirt and din, was carefully swathed in the
odds and ends of habits and humours which belonged to
a maiden lady of a whimsical, irrational, and self-indul-
gent temper. Miss Tyler, when not prepared for company, wandered about the house—a faded beauty—in the
most faded and fluttering of costumes ; but in her rags
she was spotless. To preserve herself and her worldly
gear from the dust, for ever floating and gathering in this
our sordid atmosphere, was the business of her life. Her
acquaintances she divided into the clean and the unclean—
the latter class being much the more numerous. Did one
of the unclean take a seat in her best room, the infected
chair must be removed to the garden to be aired. But
did he seat himself in Miss Tyler's own armchair,
pressing his abominable person into Miss Tyler's own
cushion, then passionate were her dismay and despair.
To her favourites she was gracious and high-bred, regaling
them with reminiscences of Lady Bateman, and with her
views on taste, Shakspere, and the musical glasses. For
her little nephew she invented the pretty recreation of
pricking playbills; all capital letters were to be illumi-

nated with pin-holes ; it was not a boisterous nor an un-
genteel sport. At other times the boy would beguile the
hours iu the garden, making friends with flowers and
insects, or looking wistfully towards that sham castle on
Claverton Hill, seat of romantic mystery, but, alas ! two
miles away, and therefore beyond the climbing powers of
a refined gentlewoman. Southey's hardest daily trial was
the luxurious morning captivity of his aunt's bed ; still
at nine, at ten that lady lay in slumber ; the small
urchin, long perked up and broad awake, feared by sound
or stir to rouse her, and would nearly wear his little
wits away in plotting re-arrangements of the curtain-
pattern, or studying the motes at mazy play in the slant
sunbeam. His happiest season was when all other little
boys were fast asleep ; then, splendid in his gayest " jam,"
he sat beside Miss Tyler in a front row of the best part
of the theatre ; when the yawning fits had passed, he was
as open-eyed as the oldest, and stared on, filling his soul
with the spectacle, till the curtain fell.

The " great red creature," Robert Southey, had now
grown into the lean greyhound of his after-life ; his long
legs wanted to be stirring, and there were childish ambitions already at work in his head. Freedom became
dearer to him than the daintiest cage, and when at six he
returned to his father's house in Wine Street, it was with
rejoicing. Now, too, his aunt issued an edict that the
long-legged lad should be breeched ; an epoch of life was
complete. Wine Street with its freedom seemed good ;
but best of all was a visit to Grandmother Hill's pleasant
house at Bedminster. " Here I had all wholesome liberty,
all wholesome indulgence, all wholesome enjoyments ; and
the delight which I there learnt to take in rural sights
and sounds has grown up with me, and continues un-

abated to this day." And now that scrambling process
called education was to begin. A year was spent by Southey
as a day-scholar with old Mr. Foot, a dissenting minister,
whose unorthodoxy as to the doctrine of the Trinity was
in some measure compensated by sound traditional views
as to the uses of the cane. Mr. Foot, having given proof
on the back of his last and his least pupil of steadfast-
ness in the faith according to Busby, died ; and it was
decided that the boy should be placed under Thomas
Flower, who kept school at Corston, nine miles from
Bristol. To a tender mother's heart nine miles seemed a
breadth of severance cruel as an Atlantic. Mrs. Southey,
born to be happy herself, and to make others happy, had
always heretofore met her son with a smile ; now he found
her weeping in her chamber ; with an effort, such as
Southey, man and boy, always knew how to make on like
occasions, he gulped down his own rising sob, and tried
to brighten her sorrow with a smile.

A boy's first night at school is usually not a time of
mirth. The heart of the solitary little lad at Corston
sank within him. A melancholy hung about the decayed
mansion which had once known better days ; the broken
gateways, the summer-houses falling in ruins, the grass-
grown court, the bleakness of the schoolroom, ill-disguised
by its faded tapestry, depressed the spirits. Southey's
pillow was wet with tears before he fell asleep. The
master was at one with his surroundings ; he too was a
piece of worthy old humanity now decayed ; he too was
falling in untimely ruins. From the memory of happier
days, from the troubles of his broken fortune, from the
vexations of the drunken maid-servant who was now his
wife, he took refuge in contemplating the order and mo-
tions of the stars. " When he came into his desk, even

there he was thinking of the stars, and looked as if he were out of humour, not from illnature, but because his calculations were interrupted." Naturally the work of the school, such as it was, fell for the most part into the hands of Charley, Thomas Flower's son. Both father and son knew the mystery of that flamboyant penmanship admired by our ancestors, but Southey's handwriting had not yet advanced from the early rounded to the decorated style. His spelling he could look back upon with pride ; on one occasion a grand spelling tournament between the boys took place, and little Southey can hardly have failed to overthrow his taller adversaries with the posers, " crystallization" and " coterie." The household arrangements at Corston, as may be supposed, were not of the most perfect kind ; Mrs. Flower had so deep an interest in her bottle, and poor Thomas Flower in his planets. The boys each morning washed themselves, or did not, in the brook ankle-deep which ran through the yard. In autumn the brook grew deeper and more swift, and after a gale it would bring within bounds a tribute of floating apples from the neighbouring orchard. That was a merry day, also in autumn, when the boys were employed to pelt the master's walnut-trees ; Southey, too small to bear his part in the battery, would glean among the fallen leaves and twigs, inhaling the penetrating fragrance which ever after called up a vision of the brook, the hillside, and its trees. One school-boy sport—that of " conquering " with snail-shells—seems to have been the special invention of Corston. The snail-shells, not tenantless, were pressed point against point until one was broken in. A great conqueror was prodigiously prized, was treated with honourable distinction, and was not exposed to danger save in great emergencies. One who had slain his hundreds might

rank with Rodney, to see whom the boys had marched
down to the Globe inn, and for whom they had cheered
and waved their Sunday cocked hats as he passed by.
So on the whole, life at Corston had its pleasures. Chief
among its pains was the misery of Sunday evenings in
winter; then the pupils were assembled in the hall to
hear the master read a sermon, or a portion of Stack-
house's History of the Bible. "Here," writes Southey,
"I sat at the end of a long form, in sight but not within
feeling of the fire, my feet cold, my eyelids heavy as
lead, and yet not daring to close them, kept awake by
fear alone, in total inaction, and under the operation
of a lecture more soporific than the strongest sleeping
dose." While the boys' souls were thus provided for,
there was a certain negligence in matters unspiritual;
an alarm got abroad that infection was among them.
This hastened the downfall of the school; one night dis-
puting was heard between Charley and his father; in
the morning poor Flower was not to be seen, and
Charley appeared with a black eye. So came to an end
the year at Corston. Southey, aged eight, was brought
home and underwent "a three days' purgatory in brim-
stone."[1]

What Southey had gained of book-lore by his two
years' schooling was as little as could be; but he was
already a lover of literature after a fashion of his own.
A friend of Miss Tyler had presented him, as soon as he
could read, with a series of Newbery's sixpenny books
for children—*Goody Twoshoes, Giles Gingerbread*, and
the rest—delectable histories, resplendent in Dutch-gilt

---

[1] Recollections of Corston, somewhat in the manner of Goldsmith's Deserted Village, will be found in Southey's early poem,
The Retrospect.

paper. The true masters of his imagination, however,
were the players and playwrights who provided amusement
for the pleasure-loving people of Bath.   Miss Tyler was
acquainted with Colman and Sheridan and Cumberland
and Holcroft ; her talk was of actors and authors, and her
nephew soon perceived that, honoured as were both classes,
the authors were awarded the higher place.   His first
dreams of literary fame accordingly were connected with
the drama.   " ' It is the easiest thing in the world to write
a play,' said I to Miss Palmer (a friend of Aunt Tyler's),
as we were in a carriage on Redcliffe Hill one day, returning from Bristol to Bedminster. ' Is it, my dear ?' was
her reply. ' Yes,' I continued, ' for you know you have
only to think what you would say if you were in the place
of the characters, and to make them say it.' "   With such
a canon of dramatic authorship Southey began a play on
the continence of Scipio, and actually completed an act
and a half. Shakspere he read and read again ; Beaumont
and Fletcher he had gone through before he was eight
years old. Were they not great theatrical names, Miss
Tyler reasoned, and therefore improving writers for her
nephew ? and Southey had read them unharmed.   When
he visited his aunt from Corston, she was a guest with
Miss Palmer at Bath ; a covered passage led to the play-
house, and every evening the delighted child, seated between the two lady-patronesses of the stage, saw the
pageantry and heard the poetry. A little later he persuaded a schoolfellow to write a tragedy ; Ballard liked
the suggestion, but could not invent a plot ; Southey
gave him a story ; Ballard approved, but found a difficulty
in devising names for the *dramatis personæ ;* Southey
supplied a list of heroic names ; they were just what
Ballard wanted—but he was at a loss to know what

the characters should say.   "I made the same attempt,"
continues Southey, "with another schoolfellow, and with
no better success.   It seemed to me very odd that they
should not be able to write plays as well as to do their
lessons."

The ingenious Ballard was an ornament of the school of
William Williams, whither Southey was sent as a day-
boarder after the catastrophe of Corston.   Under the care
of this kindly, irascible, little, bewigged old Welshman,
Southey remained during four years.   Williams was not
a model schoolmaster, but he was a man of character and
of a certain humorous originality.   In two things he believed with all the energy of his nature—in his own
spelling-book printed for his own school, and in the
Church Catechism.   Latin was left to the curate; when
Southey reached Virgil, old Williams, delighted with
classical attainments rare among his pupils, thought of
taking the boy into his own hands, but his little
Latin had faded from his brain; and the curate himself
seemed to have reached his term in the *Tityre tu patulæ
recubans sub tegmine fagi*, so that to Southey, driven round
and round the pastoral paddock, the names of Tityrus
and Melibœus became for ever after symbols of *ennui*.
No prosody was taught; "I am," said Southey, "at this
day as liable to make a false quantity as any Scotchman."
The credit, however, is due to Williams of having discovered in his favourite pupil a writer of English prose.
One day each boy of a certain standing was called upon
to write a letter on any subject he pleased; never had
Southey written a letter except the formal one dictated at
Corston which began with "Honoured Parents"; he cried
for perplexity and vexation; but Williams encouraged
him, and presently a description of Stonehenge filled his

slate. The old man was surprised and delighted; a less amiable feeling possessed Southey's schoolfellows; a plan was forthwith laid for his humiliation—could he tell them, fine scholar that he was, what the letters *i. e.* stand for? Southey, never lacking in courage, drew a bow at a venture : for John the Evangelist.

The old Welshman, an original himself, had an odd following of friends and poor retainers. There was the crazy rhymester known as " Dr. Jones " ; tradition darkly related that a dose of cantharides administered by waggish boys of a former generation had robbed him of his wits. " The most celebrated *improvisatore* was never half so vain of his talent as this queer creature, whose little figure of some five-feet-two I can perfectly call to mind, with his suit of rusty black, his more rusty wig, and his old cocked hat. Whenever he entered the school-room he was greeted with a shout of welcome." There was also Pullen the breeches-maker, a glorious fellow, brimful of vulgarity, prosperity, and boisterous good-nature ; above all, an excellent hand at demanding a half-holiday. A more graceful presence, but a more fleeting, was that of Mrs. Estan, the actress, who came to learn from the dancing-master her *minuet de la cour* in The Belle's Stratagem. Southey himself had to submit to lessons in dancing; Tom Madge, his constant partner, had limbs that went every way; Southey's limbs would go no way ; the spectacle presented by their joint endeavours was one designed for the pencil of Cruikshank. In the art of reading aloud Miss Tyler had herself instructed her nephew, probably after the manner of the most approved tragedy queens. The grand style did not please honest Williams. " Who taught you to read?" he asked scornfully. " My aunt," answered Southey. " Then give my compliments to your

aunt, and tell her that my old horse, that has been dead
these twenty years, could have taught you as well "—a
message which her nephew with the appalling frankness
of youth delivered, and which was never forgotten.

While Southey was at Corston, his grandmother died ;
the old lady with the large, clear, brown, bright eyes,
seated in her garden, was no more to be seen, and the
Bedminster house, after a brief occupation by Miss Tyler,
was sold.   Miss Tyler spoke of Bristol society with a
disdainful sniff ; it was her choice to wander for a while
from one genteel watering-place to another.   When
Williams gave Southey his first summer holidays, he
visited his aunt at Weymouth.   The hours spent there
upon the beach were the most spiritual hours of Southey's
boyhood ; he was for the first time in face of the sea—
the sea vast, voiceful, and mysterious.   Another epoch-
making event occurred about the same time ; good Mrs.
Dolignon, his aunt's friend, gave him a book—the first
which became his very own since that present of the
toy-books of Newbery.   It was Hoole's translation of
Tasso's *Gerusalemme Liberata ;* in it a world of poetical
adventure was opened to the boy.   The notes to Tasso
made frequent reference to Ariosto ; Bull's Circulating
Library at Bath—a Bodleian to Southey—supplied him
with the version, also by Hoole, of the *Orlando Furioso ;*
here was a forest of old romance in which to lose himself.
But a greater discovery was to come ; searching the notes
again, Southey found mention made of Spenser, and
certain stanzas of Spenser's chief poem were quoted.
" Was the *Faerie Queene* on Bull's shelves ? "   " Yes,"
was the answer, " they had it, but it was in obsolete
language, and the young gentleman would not understand
it."   The young gentleman, who had already gone through

Beaumont and Fletcher, was not daunted; he fell to with
the keenest relish, feeling in Spenser the presence of
something which was lacking in the monotonous couplets
of Hoole, and charming himself unaware with the music
of the stanza.　Spenser, "not more sweet than pure, and
not more pure than wise,"

High Priest of all the Muses' mysteries,[2]

was henceforth accepted by Southey as his master.

When Miss Tyler had exhausted her friends' hospitality,
and had grown tired of lodgings, she settled in a pleasant
suburban nook at Bristol; but having a standing quarrel
with Thomas Southey, her sister's brother-in-law, she
would never set foot in the house in Wine Street, and she
tried to estrange her nephew, as far as possible, from his
natural home.　Her own brother William, a half-witted
creature, she brought to live with her.　"The Squire," as
he was called, was hardly a responsible being, yet he had
a sort of *half-saved* shrewdness, and a memory stored with
old saws, which, says Southey, "would have qualified
him, had he been born two centuries earlier, to have worn
motley, and figured with a cap and bells and a bauble
in some baron's hall."　A saying of his, "Curses are
like young chickens, they always come home to roost,"
was remembered by Southey in after-years, and when it
was turned into Greek by Coleridge to serve as motto
to *The Curse of Kehama*, a mysterious reference was
given—Αποφθ. Ανεκ. του Γυλίελ. του Μητ.　With
much beer-swilling and tobacco-chewing, premature old
age came upon him.　He would sit for hours by the
kitchen fire, or on warm days in the summer-house, his

---

[2] Carmen Nuptiale: Proem, 18.

eyes intently following the movements of the neighbours.
He loved to play at marbles with his nephew, and at loo
with Miss Tyler; most of all he loved to be taken to the
theatre. The poor Squire had an affectionate heart; he
would fondle children with tenderness, and at his
mother's funeral his grief was overwhelming. A companion of his own age Southey found in Shadrach Weekes,
the boy of all work, a brother of Miss Tyler's maid.
Shad and his young master would scour the country in
search of violet and cowslip roots, and the bee and fly
orchis, until wood and rock by the side of the Avon had
grown familiar and had grown dear; and now, instead of
solitary pricking of play-bills, Southey set to work, with
the help of Shad, to make and fit up such a theatre for
puppets as would have been the pride even of Wilhelm
Meister.

But fate had already pronounced that Southey was to
be poet, and not player. Tasso and Ariosto and Spenser
claimed him, or so he dreamed. By this time he
had added to his epic cycle Pope's *Homer* and Mickle's
Lusiad. That prose romance, embroidered with sixteenth-
century affectations, but with a true chivalric sentiment
at its heart, Sidney's *Arcadia*, was also known to him.
He had read Arabian and mock-Arabian tales; he had
spent the pocket-money of many weeks on a Josephus,
and he had picked up from Goldsmith something of
Greek and Roman history. So breathed upon by poetry,
and so furnished with erudition, Southey, at twelve years
old, found it the most natural thing in the world to become
an epic poet. His removal from the old Welshman's
school having been hastened by that terrible message
which Miss Tyler could not forgive, Southey, before pro-
ceeding to Westminster, was placed for a year under a

clergyman, believed to be competent to carry his pupils
beyond Tityrus and Melibœus. But, except some skill
in writing English themes, little was gained from this
new tutor. The year, however, was not lost. "I do not
remember," Southey writes, "in any part of my life to
have been so conscious of intellectual improvement . . .
an improvement derived not from books or instruction,
but from constantly exercising myself in English verse."
"Arcadia" was the title of his first dream-poem; it was
to be grafted upon the *Orlando Furioso*, with a new hero,
and in a new scene; this dated from his ninth or tenth
year, and some verses were actually composed. The epic
of the Trojan Brutus and that of King Richard III. were
soon laid aside, but several folio sheets of an *Egbert*
came to be written. The boy's pride and ambition were
solitary and shy; one day he found a lady, a visitor of
Miss Tyler's, with the sacred sheets of *Egbert* in her
hand; her compliments on his poem were deeply resented;
and he determined henceforth to write his epics in a
private cipher. Heroic epistles, translations from Latin
poetry, satires, descriptive and moral pieces, a poem in
dialogue exhibiting the story of the Trojan war, followed
in rapid succession; last, a "Cassibelan," of which
three books were completed. Southey, looking back
on these attempts, notices their deficiency in plan, in
construction. "It was long before I acquired this power
—not fairly, indeed, till I was about five or six and
thirty; and it was gained by practice, in the course of
which I learnt to perceive wherein I was deficient."

One day in February, 1788, a carriage rumbled out of
Bath, containing Miss Palmer, Miss Tyler, and Robert
Southey, now a tall lank boy with high-poised head, brown
curling hair, bright hazel eyes, and an expression of ardour

and energy about the lips and chin.   The ladies were
on their way to London for some weeks' diversion, and
Robert Southey was on his way to school at Westminster.
For a while he remained an inconvenient appendage of
his aunt's, wearying of the great city, longing for Shad
and the carpentry, and the Gloucester meadows and the
Avon cliffs, and the honest eyes and joyous bark of poor
Phillis.   April the first—ominous morning—arrived;
Southey was driven to Dean's Yard; his name was duly
entered; his boarding-house determined; his tutor chosen;
farewells were said, and he found himself in a strange
world, alone.

CHAPTER II.

WESTMINSTER, OXFORD, PANTISOCRACY, AND MARRIAGE.

OF Southey during his four years at Westminster we know little ; his fragment of autobiography, having brought him to the school, soon comes to an untimely close ; and for this period we possess no letters. But we know that these were years which contributed much to form his intellect and character ; we know that they were years of ardour and of toil ; and it is certain that now, as heretofore, his advance was less dependent on what pastors and masters did for him than on what he did for himself. The highest scholarship—that which unites precision with breadth, and linguistic science with literary feeling—Southey never attained in any foreign tongue, except perhaps in the Portuguese and the Spanish. Whenever the choice lay between pausing to trace out a law of language, or pushing forward to secure a good armful of miscellaneous facts, Southey preferred the latter. With so many huge structures of his own in contemplation, he could not gather too much material nor gather it too quickly. Such fortitude as goes to make great scholars he possessed ; his store of patience was inexhaustible ; but he could be patient only in pursuit of his proper objects. He could never learn a language in regular fashion ; the best grammar, he said, was always the shortest. Southey's acquaintance with

Greek never got beyond that stage at which Greek, like
fairy gold, is apt to slip away of a sudden unless kept
steadfastly in view ; nearly all the Greek he had learnt at
Westminster he forgot at Oxford.   A monkish legend in
Latin of the Church, or a mediæval Latin chronicle he
could follow with the run of the eye ; but had he at any
season of his manhood been called on to write a page of
Latin prose, it would probably have resembled the French
in which he sometimes sportively addressed his friends by
letter, and in which he uttered himself valiantly while
travelling abroad.

Southey brought to Westminster an imagination stored
with the marvels and the beauty of old romance.   He
left it skilled in the new sentiment of the time—a sentiment which found in Werther and Eloisa its dialect, high-
pitched, self-conscious, rhapsodical, and not wholly real.
His bias for history was already marked before he entered
the school ; but his knowledge consisted of a few clusters
of historical facts grouped around the subjects of various
projected epics, and dotting at wide distances and almost
at random the vast expanse of time.   Now he made acquaintance with that book which more than any other
displays the breadth, the variety, and the interdependence
of the visible lives of nations.   Gibbon's *Decline and
Fall* leaves a reader cold who cares only to quicken his
own inmost being by contact with what is most precious
in man's spiritual history ; one chapter of Augustine's
Confessions, one sentence of the Imitation—each a live
coal from off the altar—will be of more worth to such
an one than all the mass and laboured majesty of Gibbon.
But one who can gaze with a certain impersonal regard
on the spectacle of the world will find the Decline and
Fall of the Roman Empire, more than almost any other

single book, replenish and dilate the mind.   In it Southey
viewed for the first time the sweep, the splendour, the
coils, the mighty movement of the stream of human
affairs.

Southey's ambition on entering Westminster was to
have the friendship of the youths who had acted in the
last Westminster Play, and whose names he had seen in
the newspaper.   Vain hope ! for they, already preparing
to tie their hair in tails, were looking onward to the
great world, and had no glance to cast on the unnoted
figures of the under-fourth.   The new-comer, according
to a custom of the school, was for a time effaced, ceasing
to exist as an individual entity, and being known only
as "shadow" of the senior boy chosen to be "substance" to him during his noviciate.   Southey accepted
his effacement the more willingly because George Strachey,
his substance, had a good face and a kindly heart; un-
luckily—Strachey boarding at home—they were parted
each night.   A mild young aristocrat, joining little with
the others, was head of the house, and Southey, unpro-
tected by his chief, stood exposed to the tyranny of a
fellow-boarder bigger and brawnier than himself, who
would souse the ears of his sleeping victim with water,
or on occasions let fly the porter-pot or the poker at his
head.   Aspiring beyond these sallies to a larger and freer
style of humour, he attempted one day to hang Southey
out of an upper window by the leg; the pleasantry was
taken ill by the smaller boy, who offered an effectual
resistance, and soon obtained his remove to another
chamber.   Southey's mature judgment of boarding-
school life was not on the whole favourable; yet
to Westminster he owed two of his best and dearest
possessions—the friendship of C. W. W. Wynn, whose

generous loyalty alone made it possible for Southey to
pursue literature as his profession, and the friendship, no
less precious, of Grosvenor Bedford, lasting green and
fresh from boyhood until both were white-haired venerable men.

Southey's interest in boyish sports was too slight to
beguile him from the solitude needful for the growth of
a poet's mind. He had thoughts of continuing Ovid's
Metamorphoses ; he planned six books to complete the
Faery Queen, and actually wrote some cantos; already
the subject of *Madoc* was chosen. And now a gigantic
conception, which at a later time was to bear fruit in
such poems as *Thalaba* and *Kehama*, formed itself in his
mind. " When I was a schoolboy at Westminster," he
writes, " I frequented the house of a schoolfellow who
has continued till this day to be one of my most intimate
and dearest friends. The house was so near Dean's Yard
that it was hardly considered as being out of our pre-
scribed bounds ; and I had free access to the library, a
well-stored and pleasant room. . . . . looking over the
river. There many of my truant hours were delightfully
spent in reading Picart's *Religious Ceremonies.* The
book impressed my imagination strongly ; and before I
left school I had formed the intention of exhibiting all
the more prominent and poetical forms of mythology,
which have at any time obtained among mankind, by
making each the groundwork of an heroic poem." Southey's
huge design was begotten upon his *pia mater* by a folio
in a library. A few years earlier Wordsworth, a boy of
fourteen, walking between Hawkshead and Ambleside,
noticed the boughs and leaves of an oak-tree intensely
outlined in black against a bright western sky. " That
moment," he says, " was important in my poetical history,

for I date from it my consciousness of the infinite variety of natural appearances which had been unnoticed by the poets of any age or country, so far as I was acquainted with them ; and I made a resolution to supply in some degree the deficiency." Two remarkable incidents in the history of English poetry, and each with something in it of a typical character.

At Westminster Southey obtained his first literary profits—the guerdon of the silver penny to which Cowper alludes in his *Table Talk.* Southey's penny—exchanged for current coin in the proportion of six to one by the mistress of the boarding-house—was always awarded for English composition. But his fame among his schoolfellows was not of an early or sudden growth. In the year of Southey's entrance, some of the senior boys commenced a weekly paper called The Trifler. It imitates, with some skill, the periodical essay of the post-Johnsonian period ; there is the wide-ranging discussion on the Influence of Liberty on Genius, there is the sprightly sketch of Amelia a learned Lady, there is the moral diatribe on Deists, a Sect of Infidels most dangerous to Mankind, there are the letters from Numa and from Infelix, there is the Eastern apologue beginning, "In the city of Bassora lived Zaydor, the son of Al-Zored." Southey lost no time in sending to the editor his latest verses ; a baby sister, Margaretta, had just died, and Southey expressed in elegy a grief which was real and keen. "The Elegy signed B. is received"—so Mr. Timothy Touchstone announced on the Saturday after the manuscript had been dropped into the penny post. The following Saturday— anxiously expected—brought no poem, but another announcement : "The Elegy by B. must undergo some Alterations ; a Liberty I must request all my Correspondents to permit me to take." "After this," says Southey, "I looked for its appearance anxiously but in vain." Happily no one sought to discover B., or supposed that he was one with the curly-headed boy of the under-fourth.

If authorship has its hours of disappointment, it has compensating moments of glory and of joy. The Trifler, having lived to the age of ten months, deceased. In 1792 Southey, now a great boy, with Strachey, his sometime "substance," and his friends Wynn and Bedford, planned a new periodical of ill-omened name, The Flagellant. "I well remember my feelings," he writes, "when the first number appeared. . . . . . . It was Bedford's writing, but that circumstance did not prevent me from feeling that I was that day borne into the world as an author, and if ever my head touched the stars while I walked upon the earth, it was then. . . . . . In all London there was not so vain, so happy, so elated a creature as I was that day." From that starry altitude he soon descended. The subject of an early number of The Flagellant was flogging; the writer was Robert Southey. He was full of Gibbon at the time, and had caught some of Voltaire's manner of poignant irony. Rather for disport of his wits than in the character of a reformer, the writer of number five undertook to prove from the ancients and the Fathers that flogging was an invention of the Devil. During Southey's life the devil received many insults at his hands ; his horns, his hoofs, his teeth, his tail, his moral character were painfully referred to ; and the devil took it, like a sensible fiend, in good part. Not so Dr. Vincent ; the preceptorial dignity was impugned by some unmannerly brat; a bulwark of the British Constitution was at stake. Dr. Vincent made haste to prosecute the publisher for libel. Matters having taken unexpectedly so serious a turn, Southey came forward, avowed himself the writer, and with some sense of shame in yielding to resentment so unwarranted and so dull, he offered his apology. The head master's wrath still held on its way, and Southey was privately expelled.

All Southey's truant hours were not passed among folios adorned with strange sculptures. In those days even St. Peter's College, Westminster, could be no little landlocked bay—silent, secure, and dull. To be in London was to be among the tides and breakers of the world. Every post brought news of some startling or significant event. Now it was that George Washington had been elected first President of the American Republic ; now that the States-General were assembled at Versailles ; now that Paris, delivered from her night-mare towers of the Bastille, breathed free ; now that Brissot was petitioning for dethronement. The main issues of the time were such as to try the spirits. Southey, who was aspiring, hopeful, and courageous, did not hesitate in choosing a side ; a new dawn was opening for the world, and should not his heart have its portion in that dawn ?

The love of our own household which surrounds us like the air, and which seems inevitable as our daily meat and drink, acquires a strange preciousness when we find that the world can be harsh. The expelled Westminster boy returned to Bristol, and faithful Aunt Tyler welcomed him home ; Shad did not avert his face, and Phillis looked up at him with her soft spaniel eyes. But Bristol also had its troubles ; the world had been too strong for the poor linen-draper in Wine Street ; he had struggled to maintain his business, but without success ; his fortune was now broken and his heart broke with it. In some respects it was well for Southey that his father's affairs

gave him definite realities to attend to, for in the quiet
and vacancy of the days in Miss Tyler's house his heart
took unusual heats and chills, and even his eager verse-
writing could not allay the excitement nor avert the
despondent fit.   When Michaelmas came, Southey went
up to Oxford to matriculate; it was intended that he
should enter at Christ Church, but the dean had heard of
the escapade at Westminster; there was a laying of big-
wigs together over that adventure, and the young rebel
was rejected; to be received, however, by Balliol College.
But to Southey it mattered little at the time whether he
were of this college or of that; a summons had reached
him to hasten to Bristol that he might follow his father's
body to the grave, and now his thoughts could not but
cling to his mother in her sorrow and her need.

"I left Westminster," says Southey, "in a perilous
state—a heart full of poetry and feeling, a head full of
Rousseau and Werther, and my religious principles shaken
by Gibbon: many circumstances tended to give me a
wrong bias, none to lead me right, except adversity, the
wholesomest of all discipline." The young republican
went up to chambers in Rat Castle—since departed—near
the head of Balliol Grove, prepared to find in Oxford the
seat of pedantry, prejudice, and aristocracy; an airy sense
of his own enlightenment and emancipation possessed
him.   He has to learn to pay respect to men "remarkable
only for great wigs and little wisdom."   He finds it
"rather disgraceful at the moment when Europe is
on fire with freedom—when man and monarch are contending—to sit and study Euclid and Hugo Grotius."
Beside the enthusiasm proper in Southey's nature, there
was at this time an enthusiasm prepense.   He had learnt
from his foreign masters the language of hyper-sensibility;

his temperament was nervous and easily wrought upon ;
his spirit was generous and ardent. Like other youths
with a facile literary talent before finding his true self,
he created a number of artificial selves, who uttered for
him his moralizings and philosophizings, who declaimed for
him on liberty, who dictated long letters of sentimental
platitudes, and who built up dream-fabrics of social and
political reforms, chiefly for the pleasure of seeing how
things might look in " the brilliant colours of fancy, nature,
and Rousseau."   In this there was no insincerity, though
there was some unreality.   " For life," he says, " I have
really a very strong predilection," and the buoyant energy
within him delayed the discovery of the bare facts of
existence ; it was so easy and enjoyable to become in turn
sage, reformer, and enthusiast.   Or perhaps we ought to
say that all this time there was a real Robert Southey,
strong, upright, ardent, simple ; and although this was
quite too plain a person to serve the purposes of epistolary
literature, it was he who gave their cues to the various
ideal personages.   This at least may be affirmed—all
Southey's unrealities were of a pure and generous cast ;
never was his life emptied of truth and meaning, and made
in the deepest degree phantasmal by a secret shame
lurking under a fair show.   The youth Milton, with his
grave upbringing, was happily not in the way of catching
the trick of sentimental phrases ; but even Milton at
Cambridge, the lady of his College, was not more clean
from spot or blemish than was Southey amid the vulgar
riot and animalisms of young Oxford.

Two influences came to the aid of Southey's instinctive
modesty, and confirmed him in all that was good.   One
was his friendship with Edmund Seward, too soon taken
from him by death.   The other was his discipleship to a

great master of conduct. One in our own day has
acknowledged the largeness of his debt to

> That halting slave, who in Nicopolis
> Taught Arrian, when Vespasian's brutal son
> Clear'd Rome of what most shamed him.

Epictetus came to Southey precisely when such a master
was needed; other writers had affected him through his
imagination, through his nervous sensibility; they had
raised around him a luminous haze; they had plunged
him deeper in illusion. Now was heard the voice of a
conscience speaking to a conscience; the manner of speech
was grave, unfigured, calm; above all it was real, and the
words bore in upon the hearer's soul with a quiet resistless-
ness. He had allowed his sensitiveness to set up what
excitements it might please in his whole moral frame; he
had been squandering his emotions; he had been indulging in a luxury and waste of passion. Here was a
tonic and a styptic. Had Southey been declamatory
about freedom? The bondsman Epictetus spoke of freedom also, and of how it might be obtained. Epictetus, like
Rousseau, told of a life according to nature; he commended
simplicity of manners. But Rousseau's simplicity, notwithstanding that homage which he paid to the will,
seemed to heat the atmosphere with strange passion,
seemed to give rise to new curiosities and refinements of
self-conscious emotion. Epictetus showed how life could
be simplified indeed by bringing it into obedience to a
perfect law. Instead of a quietism haunted by feverish
dreams,—duty, action, co-operation with God. "Twelve
years ago," wrote Southey in 1806, "I carried Epictetus in my pocket till my very heart was ingrained
with it, as a pig's bones become red by feeding him

upon madder. And the longer I live, and the more
I learn, the more am I convinced that Stoicism, properly
understood, is the best and noblest of systems." Much
that Southey gained from Stoicism he kept throughout
his whole life, tempered, indeed, by the influences of
a Christian faith, but not lost. He was no metaphysician, and a master who had placed metaphysics first and
morals after would hardly have won him for a disciple;
but a lofty ethical doctrine spoke to what was deepest and
most real in his nature. To trust in an over-ruling Providence, to accept the disposal of events not in our own
power with a strenuous loyalty to our Supreme Ruler, to
hold loose by all earthly possessions even the dearest, to
hold loose by life itself while putting it to fullest use—these
lessons he first learnt from the Stoic slave, and he
forgot none of them. But his chief lesson was the large
one of self-regulation, that it is a man's prerogative to
apply the reason and the will to the government of conduct
and to the formation of character.

By the routine of lectures and examinations Southey
profited little; he was not driven into active revolt, and
that was all. His tutor, half a democrat, surprised him
by praising America, and asserting the right of every
country to model its own forms of government. He
added, with a pleasing frankness which deserves to be
imitated, "Mr. Southey, you won't learn anything by
my lectures, sir; so, if you have any studies of your own,
you had better pursue them." Of all the months of his
life, those passed at Oxford, Southey declared, were the
most unprofitable. " All I learnt was a little swimming
. . . and a little boating . . . I never remember to have
dreamt of Oxford,—a sure proof how little it entered
into my moral being; of school, on the contrary, I dream

perpetually." The miscellaneous society of workers,
idlers, dunces, bucks, men of muscle and men of money,
did not please him; he lacked what Wordsworth calls
"the congregating temper that pervades our unripe years."
One or two friends he chose, and grappled them to his
heart; above all, Seward, who abridged his hours of
sleep for sake of study, whose drink was water, whose
breakfast was dry bread; then, Wynn and Lightfoot.
With Seward he sallied forth, in the Easter vacation,
1793, for a holiday excursion; passed with "the stupidity
of a democratic philosopher," the very walls of Blenheim,
without turning from the road to view the ducal palace;
lingered at Evesham, and wandered through its ruined
Abbey, indulging in some passable mediæval romancing;
reached Worcester and Kidderminster. "We returned
by Bewdley; there is an old mansion, once Lord Herbert's,
now mouldering away, in so romantic a situation, that I
soon lost myself in dreams of days of yore,—the tapestried
room—the listed fight—the vassal-filled hall—the hospi-
table fire—the old baron and his young daughter—these
formed a most delightful day-dream." The youthful
democrat did not suspect that such day-dreams were
treasonable—a hazardous caressing of the wily enchantress
of the past; in his pocket he carried Milton's *Defence*,
which may have been his amulet of salvation. Many and
various elements could mingle in young brains a-seethe
with revolution and romanticism. The fresh air and
quickened blood at least put Southey into excellent
spirits. "We must walk over Scotland; it will be an
adventure to delight us all the remainder of our lives: we
will wander over the hills of Morven, and mark the
driving blast, perchance bestrodden by the spirit of
Ossian!"

Among visitors to the Wye, in July, 1793, were
William Wordsworth, recently returned from France,
and Robert Southey, holiday-making from Oxford; they
were probably unacquainted with each other at that time
even by name. Wordsworth has left an undying
memorial of his tour in the poem written near Tintern
Abbey, five years later. Southey was drawing a long
breath before he uttered himself in some thousands of
blank verses. The father of his friend Bedford resided
at Brixton Causeway, about four miles on the Surrey side
of London; the smoke of the great city hung heavily
beyond an intervening breadth of country; shady lanes
led to the neighbouring villages; the garden was a sunny
solitude where flowers opened and fruit grew mellow, and
bees and birds were happy. Here Southey visited his
friend; his nineteenth birthday came; on the following
morning he planted himself at the desk in the garden
summer-house; morning after morning quickly passed;
and by the end of six weeks *Joan of Arc*, an epic poem
in twelve books, was written. To the subject Southey
was attracted primarily by the exalted character of his
heroine; but apart from this it possessed a twofold interest
for him—England in 1793 was engaged in a war against
France, a war hateful to all who sympathized with the
Republic; Southey's epic was a celebration of the glories
of French patriotism, a narrative of victory over the
invader. It was also chivalric and mediæval; the
sentiment which was transforming the word Gothic, from
a term of reproach to a word of vague yet mastering
fascination, found expression in the young poet's treatment
of the story of Joan of Arc. Knight and hermit, prince
and prelate, doctors seraphic and irrefragable with their
pupils, meet in it; the castle and the cathedral confront

one another : windows gleam with many-coloured light
streaming through the rich robes of saint and prophet ; a
miracle of carven tracery branches overhead ; upon the
altar burns the mystic lamp.

The rough draft of *Joan* was hardly laid aside when
Southey's sympathies with the revolutionary movement
in France, strained already to the utmost point of tension,
were fatally rent. All his faith, all his hope were given
to the Girondin party, and from the Girondins he
had singled out Brissot as his ideal of political courage,
purity, and wisdom. Brissot, like himself, was a disciple
of Jean Jacques ; his life was austere ; he had suffered on
behalf of freedom. On the day when the Bastille was
stormed, its keys were placed in Brissot's hands ; it was
Brissot who had determined that war should be declared
against the foreign foes of the Republic. But now the
Girondins—following hard upon Marie Antoinette—were
in the death-carts ; they chanted their last hymn of liberty,
ever growing fainter while the axe lopped head after head ;
and Brissot was among the martyrs (Oct. 31, 1793).
Probably no other public event so deeply affected Southey.
" I am sick of the world," he writes, " and discontented
with every one in it. The murder of Brissot has completely
harrowed up my faculties. . . . . I look round the world
and everywhere find the same spectacle—the strong tyran-
nizing over the weak, man and beast. . . . . There is no
place for virtue."

After this, though Southey did not lose faith in democratic principles, he averted his eyes for a time from France :
how could he look to butchers who had shed blood which
was the very life of liberty, for the realization of his
dreams ? And whither should he look ? Had he but
ten thousand republicans like himself, they might repeople

Greece and expel the Turk.   Being but one, might not
Cowley's fancy, a cottage in America, be transformed into
a fact: "three rooms . . . . and my only companion
some poor negro whom I have bought on purpose to
emancipate"? Meanwhile he occupied a room in Aunt
Tyler's house, and, instead of swinging the axe in some
forest primeval, amused himself with splitting a wedge of
oak in company with Shad, who might perhaps serve for
the emancipated negro. Moreover, he was very diligently
driving his quill: "I have finished transcribing *Joan*,
and have bound her in marble paper with green ribbons,
and am now copying all my remainables to carry to
Oxford. Then once more a clear field, and then another
epic poem, and then another." Appalling announcement!
"I have accomplished a most arduous task, transcribing
all my verses that appear worth the trouble, except letters ;
of these I took one list—another of my pile of stuff and
nonsense—and a third of what I have burnt and lost; upon
an average 10,000 verses are burnt and lost, the same
number preserved, and 15,000 worthless." Such sad
mechanic exercise dulled the ache in Southey's heart;
still "the visions of futurity," he finds, "are dark and
gloomy, and the only ray that enlivens the scene beams
on America."

To Balliol Southey returned, and if the future of the
world seemed perplexing, so also did his individual future.
His school and college expenses were borne by Mrs.
Southey's brother, the Rev. Herbert Hill, chaplain to
the British Factory at Lisbon.   In him the fatherless
youth found one who was both a friend and a father.
Holbein's portrait of Sir Thomas More in his best years,
might have passed for that of Mr. Hill; there was the
same benign thoughtfulness in his aspect, the same earnest

D

calm, the same brightness and quietness, the same serene and
cheerful strength.　He was generous and judicious, learned
and modest, and his goodness carried authority with it.
Uncle Hill's plan had been that Southey, like himself,
should become an English clergyman.　But though he might
have preached from an Unitarian pulpit, Southey could
not take upon himself the vows of a minister of the Church
of England.　It would have instantly relieved his mother
had he entered into orders.　He longed that this were
possible, and went through many conflicts of mind, and
not a little anguish.　"God knows I would exchange
every intellectual gift which He has blessed me with, for
implicit faith to have been able to do this ; " but it could
not be.　To bear the reproaches, gentle yet grave, of his
uncle was hard ; to grieve his mother was harder.　Southey
resolved to go to the anatomy school, and fit himself to
be a doctor.　But he could not overcome his strong repugnance to the dissecting-room ; it expelled him whether
he would or no ; and all the time literature with still
yet audible voice was summoning him.　Might he not
obtain some official employment in London, and also
pursue his true calling?　Beside the desire of pleasing
his uncle, and of aiding his mother, the Stoic of twenty
had now a stronger motive for seeking some immediate
livelihood.　"I shall joyfully bid adieu to Oxford," he
writes, " . . . . and when I know my situation, unite
myself to a woman whom I have long esteemed as a sister,
and for whom I now indulge a warmer sentiment."　But
Southey's reputation as a dangerous Jacobin stood in his
way ; how could his Oxford overseers answer for the good
behaviour of a youth who spoke scornfully of Pitt?

　　The shuttles of the fates now began to fly faster, and
the threads to twist and twine.　It was June of the year

1794. A visitor from Cambridge was one day introduced
to Southey ; he seemed to be of an age near his own ;
his hair, parted in the middle, fell wavy upon his neck ;
his face, when the brooding cloud was not upon him, was
bright with an abundant promise—a promise vaguely
told in lines of the sweet full lips, in the luminous eyes,
and the forehead that was like a god's. This meeting of
Southey and Coleridge was an event which decided much
in the careers of both. In the summer days and in youth,
the meeting-time of spirits, they were drawn close to one
another. Both had confessions to make with many points
in common ; both were poets, both were democrats ; both
had hoped largely from France, and the hopes of both had
been darkened ; both were uncertain what part to take
in life. We do not know whether Coleridge quickly grew
so confidential as to tell of his recent adventure as Silas
Titus Comberbatch of the 15th Light Dragoons. But
we know that Coleridge had a lively admiration for the
tall Oxford student, a person of distinction, so dignified,
so courteous, so quick of apprehension, so full of knowledge, with a glance so rapid and piercing, with a smile
so good and kind. And we know that Coleridge lost no
time in communicating to Southey the hopes that were
nearest to his heart.

Pantisocracy, word of magic, summed up these hopes.
Was it not possible for a number of men like themselves, whose way of thinking was liberal, whose characters were tried and incorruptible, to join together
and leave this old world of falling thrones and rival
anarchies, for the woods and wilds of the young republic ? One could wield an axe, another could guide a
plough. Their wants would be simple and natural ; their
toil need not be such as the slaves of luxury endure ;

where possessions were held in common, each would work for all ; in their cottages the best books would have a place ; literature and science, bathed anew in the invigorating stream of life and nature, could not but rise reanimated and purified. Each young man should take to himself a mild and lovely woman for his wife ; it would be her part to prepare their innocent food, and tend their hardy and beautiful race. So they would bring back the patriarchal age, and in the sober evening of life they would behold " colonies of independence in the undivided dale of industry." All the arguments in favour of such a scheme could not be set forth in a conversation, but Coleridge, to silence objectors, would publish a quarto volume on Pantisocracy and Aspheterism.

Southey heartily assented ; his own thoughts had, with a vague forefeeling, been pointing to America ; the unpublished epic would serve to buy a spade, a plough, a few acres of ground ; he could assuredly split timber ; he knew a mild and lovely woman for whom he indulged a warmer sentiment than that of a brother. Robert Lovell, a quaker, an enthusiast, a poet, married to the sister of Southey's Edith, would surely join them ; so would Burnett, his college friend, so perhaps would the admirable Seward. The long vacation was at hand ; being unable to take orders, or to endure the horrors of the dissecting-room, Southey must no longer remain a burden upon his uncle ; he would quit the university and prepare for the voyage.

Coleridge departed to tramp it through the romantic valleys and mountains of Wales. Southey joined his mother, who now lived at Bath, and her he soon persuaded—as a handsome and eloquent son can persuade a loving mother—that the plan of emigration was feasible ;

she even consented to accompany her boy. But his Aunt
—an *esprit borné*—was not to hear a breath of Pantisocracy ; still less would it be prudent to confess to her
his engagement to Miss Edith Fricker. His Edith was
penniless, and therefore all the dearer to Southey ; her
father had been an unsuccessful manufacturer of sugar-
pans. What would Miss Tyler, the friend of Lady Bateman, feel ? What words, what gestures, what acts would
give her feelings relief ?

When Coleridge, after his Welsh wanderings, arrived
in Bristol, he was introduced to Lovell, to Mrs. Lovell, to
Mrs. Lovell's sisters, Edith and Sarah, and Martha and
Elizabeth. Mrs. Lovell was doubtless already a pantisocrat ; Southey had probably not found it difficult to
convert Edith ; Sarah, the elder sister, who was wont to
look a mild reproof on over-daring speculations, seriously inclined to hear of pantisocracy from the lips of
Coleridge. All members of the community were to be
married. Coleridge now more than ever saw the propriety of that rule ; he was prepared to yield obedience to
it with the least possible delay. Burnett, also a pantisocrat, must also marry. Would Miss Martha Fricker join
the community as Mrs. George Burnett ? The lively
little woman refused him scornfully ; if he wanted a wife
in a hurry, let him go elsewhere. The prospects of the
reformers, this misadventure notwithstanding, from day
to day grew brighter. " This Pantisocratic scheme," so
writes Southey, " has given me new life, new hope, new
energy ; all the faculties of my mind are dilated."
Coleridge met a friend of Priestley's. But a few days
since he had toasted the great Doctor at Bala, thereby
calling forth a sentiment from the loyal parish apothecary, " I gives a sentiment, gemmen ! May all re-

publicans be gulloteened." The friend of Priestley's
said that without doubt the doctor would join them.
An American land-agent told them that for twelve men
2000*l.* would do. "He recommends the Susquehanna
from its excessive beauty and its security from hostile
Indians." The very name—Susquehanna—sounded as
if it were the sweetest of rippling rivers. Money, it
is true, as Southey admits, "is a huge evil;" but now
they are twenty-seven, and by resolute men this difficulty
can be overcome.

It was evening of the 17th of October, a dark and
gusty evening of falling rain and miry ways. Within
Aunt Tyler's house in College Green, Bristol, a storm was
bursting; she had heard it all at last—Pantisocracy,
America, Miss Fricker. Out of the house he must march;
there was the door; let her never see his face again.
Southey took his hat, looked for the last time in his life
at his aunt, then stepped out into the darkness and the
rain. "Why, sir, you ben't going to Bath at this time
of night and in this weather?" remonstrated poor Shadrach.
Even so; and with a friendly whisper master and man
parted. Southey had not a penny in his pocket, and
was lightly clad. At Lovell's he luckily found his
father's great-coat; he swallowed a glass of brandy and
set off on foot. Misery makes one acquainted with
strange road-fellows; on the way he came upon an old
man, drunk, and hardly able to stumble forward through
the night: the young pantisocrat, mindful of his fellow-
man, dragged him along nine miles amid rain and mire.
Then, with weary feet, he reached Bath, and there was
his mother to greet him with surprise, and to ask for
explanations. "Oh, Patience, Patience, thou hast often
helped poor Robert Southey, but never didst thou stand

him in more need than on Friday the 17th of October,
1794."

For a little longer the bow of hope shone in the West,
somewhere over the Susquehanna, and then it gradually
grew faint and faded. Money, that huge evil, sneered
its cold negations. The chiefs consulted, and Southey
proposed that a house and farm should be taken in Wales,
where their principles might be acted out until better
days enabled them to start upon their voyage. One
pantisocrat, at least, could be happy with Edith, brown
bread, and wild Welsh raspberries. But Coleridge
objected; their principles could not be fairly tested
under the disadvantage of an effete and adverse social
state surrounding them; besides, where was the purchase-
money to come from? how were they to live until the
gathering of their first crops? It became clear that the
realization of their plan must be postponed. The immediate problem was, How to raise 150*l.*? With such a sum
they might both qualify by marriage for membership in
the pantisocratical community. After that, the rest would
somehow follow.

How, then, to raise 150*l.*? Might they not start a new
magazine and become joint editors? The Telegraph had
offered employment to Southey. "Hireling writer to a
newspaper! 'Sdeath! 'tis an ugly title; but *n'importe.*
I shall write truth and only truth." The offer, however,
turned out to be that of a reporter's place; and his trouble-
some guest, honesty, prevented his contributing to The
True Briton. But he and Coleridge could at least
write poetry, and perhaps publish it with advantage
to themselves; and they could lecture to a Bristol
audience. With some skirmishing lectures on various
political subjects of immediate interest Coleridge began;

many came to hear them, and the applause was loud.
Thus encouraged, he announced and delivered two remarkable courses of lectures—one, A comparative view of the
English Rebellion under Charles I. and the French Revolution ; the other, On Revealed Religion, its Corrup-
tions and its Political Views. Southey did not feel
tempted to discuss the origin of evil or the principles of
revolution. He chose as his subject a view of the course
of European history from Solon and Lycurgus to the
American War. His hearers were pleased by the graceful
delivery and unassuming self-possession of the young
lecturer, and were quick to recognize the unusual range of
his knowledge, his just perception of facts, his ardour and
energy of conviction.   One lecture Coleridge begged permission to deliver in Southey's place—that on the Rise,
Progress, and Decline of the Roman Empire.   Southey
consented, and the room was thronged ; but no lecturer
appeared ; they waited ; still no lecturer.   Southey offered
an apology, and the crowd dispersed in no happy temper.
It is likely, adds that good old gossip Cottle, who tells
the story, "that at this very moment Mr. Coleridge
might have been found at No. 48, College Street, com-
posedly smoking his pipe, and lost in profound musings on
his divine Susquehannah."

The good Cottle—young in 1795, a publisher, and unhappily a poet—rendered more important service to the
two young men than that of smoothing down their ruffled
tempers after this incident.   Southey, in conjunction with
Lovell, had already published a slender volume of verse.
The pieces by Southey recall his schoolboy joys and
sorrows, and tell of his mother's tears, his father's death,
his friendship with " Urban," his love of " Ariste," lovely
maid ! his delight in old romance, his discipleship to

Rousseau. They are chiefly of interest as exhibiting the diverse literary influences to which a young writer of genius was exposed in the last quarter of the eighteenth century. Here the couplet of Pope reappears, and hard by the irregular ode as practised by Warton, the elegy as written by Gray, the unrhymed stanza which Collins's *Evening* made a fashion, the sonnet to which Bowles had lent a meditative grace, and the rhymeless measures imitated by Southey from Sayers, and afterwards made popular by his *Thalaba.* On the last page of this volume appear " Proposals for publishing by subscription *Joan of Arc ;* " but subscriptions came slowly in. One evening Southey read for Cottle some books of *Joan.* " It can rarely happen," he writes, " that a young author should meet with a bookseller as inexperienced and as ardent as himself." Cottle offered to publish the poem in quarto, to make it the handsomest book ever printed in Bristol, to give the author fifty copies for his subscribers, and fifty pounds to put forthwith into his purse. Some dramatic attempts had recently been made by Southey, *Wat Tyler,* of which we shall hear more at a later date, and the *Fall of Robespierre,* undertaken by Coleridge, Lovell, and Southey, half in sport—each being pledged to produce an act in twenty-four hours. These were now forgotten, and all his energies were given to revising and in part recasting *Joan.* In six weeks his epic had been written ; its revision occupied six months.

With summer came a great sorrow, and in the end of autumn a measureless joy. " He is dead," Southey writes, " my dear Edmund Seward ! after six weeks' suffering. . . . . You know not, Grosvenor, how I loved poor Edmund : he taught me all that I have of good. . . . . There is a strange vacancy in my heart. . . . . I have

lost a friend, and such a one !" And then characteristically come the words : " I will try, by assiduous employment, to get rid of very melancholy thoughts." Another
consolation Southey possessed : during his whole life he
steadfastly believed that death is but the removal of a
spirit from earth to heaven ; and heaven for him meant a
place where cheerful familiarity was natural, where perhaps
he himself would write more epics and purchase more
folios. As Baxter expected to meet among the saints
above Mr. Hampden and Mr. Pym, so Southey counted
upon the pleasure of having long talks with friends, of
obtaining introductions to eminent strangers ; above all,
he looked forward to the joy of again embracing his
beloved ones :—

> Often together have we talked of death ;
>   How sweet it were to see
> All doubtful things made clear ;
> How sweet it were with powers
>   Such as the Cherubim
> To view the depth of Heaven !
>   O Edmund ! thou hast first
> Begun the travel of eternity.

Autumn brought its happiness pure and deep. Mr.
Hill had arrived from Lisbon ; once again he urged his
nephew to enter the church ; but for one of Southey's
opinions the church-gate " is perjury," nor does he even
find church-going the best mode of spending his Sunday. He proposed to choose the law as his profession.
But his uncle had heard of Pantisocracy, Aspheterism,
and Miss Fricker, and said the law could wait ; he should
go abroad for six months, see Spain and Portugal, learn
foreign languages, read foreign poetry and history, rum-
mage among the books and manuscripts his uncle had col-

lected in Lisbon, and afterwards return to his Blackstone.
Southey, straightforward in all else, in love became a
Machiavel. To Spain and Portugal he would go; his mother
wished it; Cottle expected from him a volume of travels;
his uncle had but to name the day. Then he sought
Edith and asked her to promise that before he departed
she would become his wife; she wept to think that he was
going, and yet persuaded him to go; consented finally to all
that he proposed. But how was he to pay the marriage fees
and buy the wedding-ring? Often this autumn he had
walked the streets dinnerless, no pence in his pocket, no
bread and cheese at his lodgings, thinking little, however,
of dinner, for his head was full of poetry and his heart
of love. Cottle lent him money for the ring and the
licence—and Southey in after-years never forgot the kindness of his honest friend. He was to accompany his uncle,
but Edith was first to be his own; so she may honourably
accept from him whatever means he can furnish for her
support. It was arranged with Cottle's sisters that she
should live with them, and still call herself by her maiden
name. On the morning of the 14th of November, 1795,
a day sad, yet with happiness underlying all sadness,
Robert Southey was married in Redcliffe Church, Bristol,
to Edith Fricker. At the church door there was a pressure of hands, and they parted with full hearts, silently
—Mrs. Southey to take up her abode in Bristol, with the
wedding-ring upon her breast, her husband to cross the
sea. Never did woman put her happiness in more loyal
keeping.

So by love and by poetry, by Edith Fricker and by
Joan of Arc, Southey's life was being shaped. Powers
most benign leaned forward to brood over the coming
years and to bless them. It was decreed that his heart

should be no homeless wanderer ; that, as seasons went by,
children should be in his arms and upon his knees ; it was
also decreed that he should become a strong toiler among
books.   Now Pantisocracy looked faint and far ; the facts
plain and enduring of the actual world took hold of his
adult spirit.   And Coleridge complained of this, and did
not come to bid his friend farewell.

CHAPTER III.

WANDERINGS, 1795—1803.

THROUGH pastoral Somerset, through Devon amid falling leaves, then over rough Cornish roads, the coach brought Southey, cold, hungry, and dispirited, to Falmouth. No packet there for Corunna ; no packet starting before December 1st. The gap of time looked colourless and dreary, nor could even the philosophy of Epictetus lift him quite above " the things independent of the will." After a comfortless and stormy voyage, on the fifth morning the sun shone, and through a mist the barren cliffs of Galicia, with breakers tumbling at their feet, rose in sight. Who has not experienced, when first he has touched a foreign soil, how nature purges the visual nerve with lucky euphrasy ? The shadowy streets, the latticed houses, the fountains, the fragments of Moorish architecture, the Jewish faces of the men, the lustrous eyes of girls, the children gaily bedizened, the old witch-like women with brown shrivelled parchment for skin, told Southey that he was far from home. Nor at night was he permitted to forget his whereabouts ; out of doors cats were uttering soft things in most vile Spanish ; beneath his blanket, familiars, bloodthirsty as those of the Inquisition, made him their own. He was not sorry when the crazy coach, drawn by six mules, received him and his uncle, and the

journey eastward began to the shout of the muleteers
and the clink of a hundred bells.

Some eighteen days were spent upon the road to
Madrid. Had Southey not left half his life behind
him in Bristol, those December days would have been
almost wholly pleasurable. As it was they yielded a
large possession for the inner eye, and gave his heart a
hold upon this new land which, in a certain sense, became
for ever after the land of his adoption. It was pleasant
when having gone forward on foot he reached the crest
of some mountain road, to look down on broken waters
in the glen, and across to the little white-walled convent
amid its chestnuts, and back to the dim ocean; there, on
the summit, to rest with the odour of furze-blossoms and
the tinkle of goats in the air, and while the mules wound
up the long ascent to turn all this into hasty rhymes,
ending with the thought of peace and love and Edith.
Then the bells audibly approaching, and the loud-voiced
muleteer consigning his struggling team to Saint Michael
and three hundred devils; and then on to remoter hills,
or moor and swamp, or the bridge flung across a ravine,
or the path above a precipice with mist and moonlight
below. And next day some walled city with its decay-
ing towers and dim piazza, some church with its balcony
of ghastly skulls, some abandoned castle, or jasper-pillared
Moorish gateway and gallery. Nor were the little inns
and baiting-houses without compensations for their manifold discomforts. The Spanish country-folk were dirty
and ignorant, but they had a courtesy unknown to English peasants; Southey would join the group around the
kitchen fire and be, as far as his imperfect speech allowed,
one with the rustics, the carriers, the hostess, the children,
the village barber, the familiar priest, and the familiar

pigs. When chambermaid Josepha took hold of his hair
and gravely advised him never to tie it or to wear powder,
she meant simple friendliness, no more. In his recoil
from the dream of human perfectibility, Southey allowed
himself at times to square accounts with common sense
by a cynical outbreak ; but in truth he was a warm-hearted
lover of his kind. Even feudalism and Catholicism had
not utterly degraded the Spaniard. Southey thanks God
that the pride of chivalry is extinguished ; his Protestant
zeal becomes deep-dyed in presence of our Lady of Seven
Sorrows and the Holy Napkin. " Here in the words of Mary
Wollstonecraft," he writes, " ' the serious folly of Superstition stares every man of sense in the face.' " Yet Spain
has inherited tender and glorious memories ; by the
river Ezla he recalls Montemayor's wooing of his Diana ;
at Tordesillas he muses on the spot where Queen Joanna
watched by her husband's corpse, and where Padilla,
Martyr of Freedom, triumphed and endured. At length,
the travellers, accompanied by Manuel, the most viva-
cious and accomplished of barbers, drew near Madrid,
passed the miles of kneeling washerwomen and outspread
clothes on the river banks, entered the city, put up at the
Cruz de Malta, and were not ill-content to procure once
more a well-cooked supper and a clean bed.

Southey pursued with ardour his study of the Spanish
language, and could soon talk learnedly of its great writers.
The national theatres, and the sorry spectacle of bullock-
teasing, made a slighter impression upon him than did the
cloisters of the new Franciscan Convent. He had been
meditating his design of a series of poems to illustrate
the mythologies of the world ; here the whole portentous
history of St. Francis was displayed upon the walls. " Do
they believe all this, sir ? " he asked Mr. Hill. " Yes, and

a great deal more of the same kind," was the reply. "My first thought was . . . . . here is a mythology not less wild and fanciful than any of those upon which my imagination was employed, and one which ought to be included in my ambitious design." Thus Southey's atten-tion was drawn for the first time to the legendary and monastic history of the Church.

His Majesty of Spain, with his courtesans and his cour-tiers, possibly also with the Queen and her gallants, had gone westward to meet the Portuguese court upon the borders. As a matter of course, therefore, no traveller could hope to leave Madrid, every carriage, cart, horse, mule, and ass being embargoed for the royal service. The followers of the father of his people numbered seven thousand, and they advanced, devouring all before them, neither paying nor promising to pay, leaving a broad track behind as bare as that stripped by an army of locusts, with here a weeping cottager and there a smoking cork-tree for a memorial of their march. Ten days after the king's departure, Mr. Hill and his nephew succeeded in finding a buggy with two mules, and made their escape, taking with them their own larder. Their destination was Lisbon, and as they drew towards the royal party, the risk of embargo added a zest to travel hardly less piquant than that imparted by the neighbourhood of bandits. It was mid-January; the mountains shone with snow; but olive-gathering had begun in the plains; violets were in blossom, and in the air was a genial warmth. As they drove south and west, the younger traveller noted for his diary the first appearance of orange-trees, the first myrtle, the first fence of aloes. A pressure was on their spirits till Lisbon should be reached; they would not linger to watch the sad procession attending a body uncovered upon its bier;

they left behind the pilgrims to our Lady's Shrine, pious
bacchanals half-naked and half drunk, advancing to the
tune of bag-pipe and drum; then the gleam of waters
before them, a rough two hours' passage, and the weary
heads were on their pillows, to be roused before morning
by an earthquake with its sudden trembling and cracking.

Life at Lisbon was not altogether after Southey's heart.
His uncle's books and manuscripts were indeed a treasure
to explore, but Mr. Hill lived in society as well as in his
study, and thought it right to give his nephew the advantage of new acquaintances. What had the author of *Joan
of Arc*, the husband of Edith Southey, the disciple of
Rousseau, of Godwin, the Stoic, the tall, dark-eyed young
man with a certain wildness of expression in his face,
standing alone or discoursing earnestly on Industrial Com-
munities of Women—what had he to do with the *inania
regna* of the drawing-room? He cared not for cards nor for
dancing; he possessed no gift for turning the leaves on
the harpsichord, and saying the happy word at the right
moment. Southey, indeed, knew as little as possible of
music; and all through his life acted on the principle
that the worthiest use of sound without sense had been
long ago discovered by schoolboys let loose from their
tasks; he loved to create a chaos of sheer noise after
those hours during which silence had been interrupted
only by the scraping of his pen. For the rest, the sallies
of glee from a mountain brook, the piping of a thrush
from the orchard-bough, would have delighted him more
than all the trills of Sontag or the finest rapture of
Malibran. It was with some of the superiority and seriousness of a philosopher just out of his teens that he
unbent to the frivolities of the Lisbon drawing-rooms.

But if Lisbon had its vexations, the country, the climate,

E

the mountains with their streams and coolness, the odorous gardens, Tagus flashing in the sunlight, the rough bar glittering with white breakers, and the Atlantic, made amends. When April came, Mr. Hill moved to his house at Cintra, and the memories and sensations "felt in the blood and felt along the heart," which Southey brought with him to England, were especially associated with this delightful retreat. "Never was a house more completely secluded than my uncle's: it is so surrounded with lemon-trees and laurels as nowhere to be visible at the distance of ten yards. . . . . A little stream of water runs down the hill before the door, another door opens into a lemon-garden, and from the sitting-room we have just such a prospect over lemon-trees and laurels to an opposite hill as, by promising a better, invites us to walk. . . . . On one of the mountain eminences stands the Penha Convent, visible from the hills near Lisbon. On another are the ruins of a Moorish castle, and a cistern, within its boundaries, kept always full by a spring of purest water that rises in it. From this elevation the eye stretches over a bare and melancholy country to Lisbon on the one side, and on the other to the distant Convent of Mafra, the Atlantic bounding the greater part of the prospect. I never beheld a view that so effectually checked the wish of wandering."

"Lisbon, from which God grant me a speedy deliverance," is the heading of one of Southey's letters; but when the day came to look on Lisbon perhaps for the last time, his heart grew heavy with happy recollection. It was with no regretful feeling, however, that he leaped ashore, glad after all to exchange the sparkling Tagus and the lemon groves of Portugal for the mud-encumbered tide of Avon and a glimpse of British smoke. "I intend to write a

hymn," he says, "to the Dii Penates." His joy in reunion with his wife was made more rare and tender by
finding her in sorrow ; the grief was also peculiarly his own
—Lovell was dead. He had been taken ill at Salisbury, and
by his haste to reach his fireside had heightened the fever
which hung upon him. Coleridge, writing to his friend
Poole at this time, expresses himself with amiable but
inactive piety : " The widow is calm, and amused with
her beautiful infant. We are all become more religious
than we were. God be ever praised for all things."
Southey also writes characteristically : " Poor Lovell ! I
am in hopes of raising something for his widow by publishing his best pieces, if only enough to buy her a
harpsichord. . . . Will you procure me some subscribers ? " No idle conceit of serving her, for Mrs.
Lovell with her child, as well as Mrs. Coleridge with her
children, at a later time became members of the Southey
household. Already—though Coleridge might resent it—
Southey was willing to part with some vague enthusiams
which wandered in the inane of a young man's fancy, for
the sake of simple loyalties and manly tendernesses. No
one was more boyish-hearted than Southey at fifty ; but
even at twenty-two it would not have been surprising to
find grey hairs sprinkling the dark. " How does time
mellow down our opinions ! Little of that ardent enthusiasm which so lately fevered my whole character remains. I have contracted my sphere of action within
the little circle of my own friends, and even my wishes
seldom stray beyond it. . . . I want a little room to
arrange my books in, and some Lares of my own." This
domestic feeling was not a besotted contentment in narrow
interests ; no man was more deeply moved by the political
changes in his own country, by the national uprising in

the Spanish peninsula, than Southey; while seated at his desk, his intellect ranged through dim centuries of the past. But his heart needed an abiding-place, and he yielded to the bonds—strict and dear—of duty and of love which bound his own life to the lives of others.

The ambitious quarto on which Cottle prided himself not a little was now published (1796). To assign its true place to *Joan of Arc* we must remember that narrative poetry in the eighteenth century was of the slenderest dimensions and the most modest temper. Poems of description and sentiment seemed to leave no place for poems of action and passion. Delicately finished cabinet pictures like Shenstone's *Schoolmistress* and Goldsmith's *Deserted Village* had superseded fresco. The only great English epic of that century is the prose Odyssey of which Mr. Tom Jones is the hero. That estimable London merchant, Glover, had indeed written an heroic poem containing the correct number of Books; its subject was a lofty one; the sentiments were generous, the language dignified; and inasmuch as Leonidas was a patriot and a whig, true whigs and patriots bought and praised the poem. But Glover's poetry lacks the informing breath of life. His second poem, *The Athenaid*, appeared after his death and its thirty books fell plumb into the water of oblivion. It looked as if the narrative poem *à longue haleine* was dead in English literature. Cowper had given breadth, with a mingled gaiety and gravity, to the poetry of description and sentiment; Burns had made the air tremulous with snatches of pure and thrilling song; the *Lyrical Ballads* were not yet. At this moment from a provincial press *Joan of Arc* was issued. As a piece of romantic narrative it belongs to the new age of poetry; in sentiment it is revolutionary and republican; its garment of style is of the eighteenth century. Nowhere, except it be in the verses which hail "Inoculation, lovely Maid !" does the personified abstraction, galvanized into life by printer's type and poet's epithet, stalk more at large than in the unfortunate ninth book, the Vision of the Maid, which William Taylor of Norwich pronounced worthy of Dante. The critical reviews of the time were liberal in politics, and the poem was praised and bought. " Brissot murdered" was good, and " the blameless wife of Roland" atoned for some offences against taste ; there was also that notable reference to the " Almighty people " who " from their tyrant's hand dashed down the iron rod." The delegated maid is a creature overflowing with Rous-seauish sensibility; virtue, innocence, the peaceful cot, stand over against the wars and tyranny of kings, and the superstition and cruelty of prelates. Southey himself soon disrelished the youthful heats and violences of the poem; he valued it as the work which first lifted him into public view; and partly out of a kind of gratitude he rehandled the *Joan* again and again. It would furnish an instructive lesson to a young writer to note how its asperities were softened, its spasm subdued, its swelling words abated. Yet its chief interest will be perceived only by readers of the earlier text. To the second book Coleridge contributed some four hundred lines, where Platonic philosophy and protests against the Newtonian hypothesis of æther are not very appropriately brought into connexion with the shepherd-girl of Domremi. These lines disappeared from all editions after the first.[1]

[1] I find in a Catalogue of English Poetry, 1862, the following passage from an autograph letter of S. T. Coleridge, dated Bristol, July 16, 1814, then in Mr. Pickering's possession :—" I looked over the first five books of the 1st (Quarto) edition of

The neighbourhood of Bristol was for the present
Southey's home. The quickening of his blood by the
beauty, the air and sun of Southern Europe, the sense
of power imparted by his achievement in poetry,
the joy of reunion with his young wife, the joy also of
solitude among rocks and woods, combined to throw him
into a vivid and creative mood. His head was full of
designs for tragedies, epics, novels, romances, tales—
among the rest "my Oriental poem of The Destruction of
the Dom Daniel." He has a "Helicon kind of dropsy"
upon him; he had rather leave off eating than poetizing.
He was also engaged in making the promised book of travel
for Cottle; in what leisure time remained after these
employments he scribbled for The Monthly Magazine,
and to good purpose, for in eight months he had earned
no less than "seven pounds and two pair of breeches,"
which, as he observes to his brother Tom, "is not
amiss." He was resolved to be happy, and he was happy.
Now, too, the foolish estrangement on Coleridge's part
was brought to an end. Southey had been making
some acquaintance with German literature at second
hand. He had read Taylor's rendering of Bürger's
Lenore and wondered who this William Taylor was; he
had read Schiller's *Cabal and Love* in a wretched translation, finding the fifth act dreadfully affecting; he had

Joan of Arc yesterday, at Hood's request, in order to mark the
lines written by me. I was really astonished—1, at the schoolboy
wretched allegoric machinery—2, at the transmogrification of the
fanatic Virago, into a modern Novel-pawing proselyte of the Age
of Reason, a Tom Paine in petticoats, but so lovely! and in love
more dear! '*On her rubied cheek hung pity's crystal gem*'—3, at
the utter want of all rhythm in the verse, the monotony and the
dead plumb down of the pauses, and of the absence of all bone,
muscle, and sinew in the single lines."

also read Schiller's *Fiesco*. Coleridge was just back after
a visit to Birmingham, but still held off from his brother-
in-law and former friend. A sentence from Schiller, copied
on a slip of paper by Southey, with a word or two of con-
ciliation, was sent to the offended Abdiel of Pantisocracy :
" Fiesco ! Fiesco ! thou leavest a void in my bosom, which
the human race, thrice told, will never fill up." It did
not take much to melt the faint resentment of Coleridge,
and to open his liberal heart. An interview followed,
and in an hour's time, as the story is told by Coleridge's
nephew, " these two extraordinary youths were arm in
arm again."

Seven pounds and two pair of breeches are not amiss,
but pounds take to themselves wings, and fly away ;
a poet's wealth is commonly in the *paulo-post-futurum*
tense ; it therefore behoved Southey to proceed with
his intended study of the law. By Christmas he would
receive the first instalment of an annual allowance
of 160*l*. promised by his generous friend Wynn upon
coming of age ; but Southey, who had just written his
Hymn to the Penates—a poem of grave tenderness and
sober beauty—knew that those deities are exact in their
demand for the dues of fire and salt, for the firstlings
of fruits, and for offerings of fine flour. A hundred and
sixty pounds would not appease them. To London
therefore he must go, and Blackstone must become his
counsellor. But never did Sindbad suffer from the
tyrannous old man between his shoulders as Robert
Southey suffered from Blackstone. London in itself
meant deprivation of all that he most cared for ; he
loved to shape his life in large and simple lines, and
London seemed to scribble over his consciousness with
distractions and intricacies. " My spirits always sink

when I approach it. Green fields are my delight. I
am not only better in health, but even in heart, in
the country." Some of his father's love of rural
sights and sounds was in him, though hare-hunting
was not an amusement of Southey the younger; he
was as little of a sportsman as his friend Sir Thomas
More; the only murderous sport indeed which Southey
ever engaged in was that of pistol-shooting, with sand
for ammunition, at the wasps in Bedford's garden when
he needed a diversion from the wars of Talbot and
the "missioned Maid." Two pleasures of a rare kind
London offered, the presence of old friends, and the
pursuit of old books upon the stalls. But not even for
these best lures proposed by the Demon of the place
would Southey renounce

> The genial influences
> And thoughts and feelings to be found where'er
> We breathe beneath the open sky, and see
> Earth's liberal bosom.

To London, however, he would go, and would read
nine hours a day at law. Although he pleaded at times
against his intended profession, Southey really made
a strenuous effort to overcome his repugnance to legal
studies, and for a while Blackstone and *Madoc* seemed
to advance side by side. But the bent of his nature
was strong. " I commit wilful murder on my own
intellect," he writes two years later, " by drudging at
law." And the worst or the best of it was that all his
drudgery was useless. Southey's memory was of that
serviceable sieve-like kind which retains everything needful to its possessor, and drops everything which is mere
incumbrance. Every circumstance in the remotest degree
connected with the seminary of magicians in the Dom

Daniel under the roots of the sea adhered to his memory,
but how to proceed in the Court of Common Pleas was
always just forgotten since yesterday. "I am not
indolent; I loathe indolence; but, indeed, reading law
is laborious indolence—it is thrashing straw. . . . I
have given all possible attention and attempted to command volition; . . . close the book and all was gone."
In 1801, there was a chance of Southey's visiting Sicily
as secretary to some Italian Legation. "It is unfortunate," he writes to Bedford, "that you cannot come to
the sacrifice of one law book—my whole proper stock—
whom I design to take up to the top of Mount Etna,
for the express purpose of throwing him straight to
the devil. Huzza, Grosvenor! I was once afraid that I
should have a deadly deal of law to forget whenever I
had done with it; but my brains, God bless them, never
received any, and I am as ignorant as heart could wish.
The tares would not grow."

As spring advanced, impatience quickened within him;
the craving for a lonely place in sight of something green
became too strong. Why might not law be read in
Hampshire under blue skies, and also poetry be written?
Southey longed to fill his eyesight with the sea, and
with sunsets over the sea; he longed to renew that
delicious shock of plunging in salt waves which he had
last enjoyed in the Atlantic at the foot of the glorious
Arrabida mountain. Lodgings were found at Burton near
Christ Church (1797), and here took place a little Southey
family-gathering, for his mother joined them, and his
brother Tom, the midshipman, just released from a French
prison. Here too came Cottle, and there were talks about
the new volume of shorter poems; here came Lloyd, the
friend of Coleridge, himself a writer of verse, and with

Lloyd came Lamb, the play of whose letters show that
he found in Southey not only a fellow-lover of quaint
books, but also a ready smiler at quips and cranks and
twinklings of sly absurdity. And here he found John
Rickman, "the sturdiest of jovial companions," whose
clear head and stout heart were at Southey's service
whenever they were needed through all the future years.

When the holiday at Burton was at an end Southey had
for a time no fixed abode. He is now to be seen roaming
over the cliffs by the Avon, and now casting a glance
across some book-stall near Gray's Inn. In these and
subsequent visits to London he was wistful for home, and
eager to hasten back. "At last, my dear Edith, I sit
down to write to you in quiet and something like comfort. . . . My morning has been spent pleasantly, for it
has been spent alone in the library; the hours so employed pass rapidly enough, but I grow more and more
home-sick, like a spoilt child. On the 29th you may
expect me. Term opens on the 26th; after eating
my third dinner I can drive to the mail, and thirteen
shillings will be well bestowed in bringing me home
four-and-twenty hours earlier—it is not above sixpence
an hour, Edith, and I would gladly purchase an hour at
home now at a much higher price."

A visit to Norwich (1798) was pleasant and useful as
widening the circle of his literary friends. Here Southey
obtained an introduction to William Taylor, whose
translations from the German had previously attracted
his notice. Norwich at the end of the last century and
the beginning of the present was a little Academe among
provincial cities, where the *belles lettres* and mutual
admiration were assiduously cultivated. Southey saw
Norwich at its best. Among its "superior people" were

several who really deserved something better than that
vague distinction.   Chief among them was Dr. Sayers,
whom the German critics compared to Gray, who had
handled the Norse mythology in poetry, who created
the English monodrama, and introduced the rhymeless
measures followed by Southey.   He rested too soon upon
his well-earned reputation, contented himself with touching and retouching his verses, and possessing singularly
pleasing manners, abounding information and genial wit,
embellished and enjoyed society.[2]   William Taylor, the
biographer of Sayers, was a few years his junior.   He
was versed in Goethe, in Schiller, in the great Kotzebue
—Shakspere's immediate successor, in Klopstock, in the
fantastic ballad, in the new criticism, and all this at
a time when German characters were as undecipherable to
most Englishmen as Assyrian arrow-heads.   The whirligig
of time brought an odd revenge when Carlyle, thirty years
later, hailed in Taylor the first example of " the natural-
born English Philistine."   In Norwich he was known as a
model of filial virtue, a rising light of that illuminated city,
a man whose extraordinary range pointed him out as the
fit and proper person to be interrogated by any blue-stocking
lady upon topics as remote as the domestic arrangements
of the Chinese Emperor, Chim-Cham-Chow.   William
Taylor had a command of new and mysterious words ; he
shone in paradox, and would make ladies aghast by
" defences of suicide, avowals that snuff alone had rescued
him from it, information, given as certain, that ' God save
the King' was sung by Jeremiah in the temple of Solomon,"[3] with other blasphemies borrowed from the German,

[2] See Southey's article on " Dr. Sayers's Works," Quarterly
Review, Jan. 1827.
[3] Harriet Martineau: Autobiography, i. p. 300.

and too startling even for rationalistic Norwich.   Dr.
Enfield, from whose *Speaker* our fathers learnt to
recite "My name is Norval," was no longer living; he
had just departed in the odour of dilettantism.   But
solemn Dr. Alderson was here, and was now engaged in
giving away his daughter Amelia to a divorced bride-
groom, the painter Opie.   Just now Elizabeth Gurney
was listening in the Friends' Meeting-House to that
discourse which transformed her from a gay haunter of
country ball-rooms to the sister and servant of Newgate
prisoners.   The Martineaus also were of Norwich, and
upon subsequent visits the author of *Thalaba* and *Kehama*
was scrutinized by the keen eyes of a little girl—not born
at the date of his first visit—who smiled somewhat too
early and somewhat too maliciously at the airs and affectations of her native town, and whose pleasure in pricking
a wind-bag, literary, political, or religious, was only over-
exquisite.   But Harriet Martineau, who honoured courage,
purity, faithfulness, and strength, wherever they were
found, reverenced the Tory Churchman, Robert
Southey.[4]

Soon after his return from Norwich a small house was
taken at Westbury (1798), a village two miles distant from
Bristol.   During twelve happy months this continued to be
Southey's home.   " I never before or since," he says in one
of the prefaces to his collected poems, "produced so much
poetry in the same space of time."   William Taylor, by
talks about Voss and the German idylls, had set Southey
thinking of a series of English Eclogues ; Taylor also expressed his wonder that some one of our poets had not
undertaken what the French and Germans so long supported, an Almanack of the Muses, or Annual Anthology of

----

[4] See her " History of the Peace," B. vi. chap. xvi.

minor poems by various writers. The suggestion was well
received by Southey, who became editor of such annual
volumes for the years 1799 and 1800. At this period
were produced many of the ballads and short pieces which
are perhaps more generally known than any other of
Southey's writings. He had served his apprenticeship to
the craft and mystery of such verse-making in the Morning
Post, earning thereby a guinea a week, but it was not
until *Bishop Bruno* was written at Westbury that he had
the luck to hit off the right tone, as he conceived it, of
the modern ballad. The popularity of his *Mary the Maid
of the Inn*, which unhappy children got by heart, and
which some one even dramatized, was an affliction to its
author, for he would rather have been remembered as a
ballad writer in connexion with *Rudiger* and *Lord
William*. What he has written in this kind certainly
does not move the heart as with a trumpet, it does not
bring with it the dim burden of sorrow which is laid upon
the spirit by songs like those of Yarrow crooning of " old,
unhappy far-off things." But to tell a tale of fantasy
briefly, clearly, brightly, and at the same time with a
certain heightening of imaginative touches, is no common
achievement. The spectre of the murdered boy in *Lord
William* shone upon by a sudden moonbeam, and surrounded by the welter of waves is more than a picturesque
apparition ; readers of goodwill may find him a very genuine
little ghost, a stern and sad justicer. What has been
named " the lyrical cry " is hard to find in any of Southey's
shorter poems. In *Roderick* and elsewhere he takes delight in representing great moments of life when fates are
decided, but such moments are usually represented as
eminences on which will and passion wrestle in a mortal
embrace, and if the cry of passion be heard, it is often

a half-stifled death cry.   The best of Southey's shorter
poems expressing personal feelings are those which sum
up the virtue spread over seasons of life and long habitual
moods.   Sometimes he is simply sportive as a serious man
released from thought and toil may be, and at such times
the sportiveness, while genuine as a schoolboy's, is like a
schoolboy's the reverse of keen-edged ; on other occasions
he expresses simply a strong man's endurance of sorrow ;
but more often an undertone of gravity appears through
his glee, and in his sorrow there is something of solemn
joy.

All this year (1799) *Madoc* was steadily advancing, and
The Destruction of the Dom Daniel had been already
sketched in outline.   Southey was fortunate in finding an
admirable listener.   The Pneumatic Institution, established
in Bristol by Dr. Beddoes, was now under the care of a
youth lately an apothecary's apprentice at Penzance, a poet,
but still more a philosopher, " a miraculous young man."
" He is not yet twenty-one, nor has he applied to chemistry
more than eighteen months, but he has advanced with
such seven-leagued strides as to overtake everybody ;
his name is Davy "—Humphrey Davy—" the young
chemist, the young everything, the man least ostentatious,
of first talent that I have ever known."   Southey would
walk across from Westbury, an easy walk over beautiful
ground, to breathe Davy's wonder-working gas, "which
excites all possible mental and muscular energy, and
induces almost a delirium of pleasurable sensations without any subsequent dejection."   Pleased to find scientific
proof that he possessed a poet's fine susceptibility, he
records that the nitrous oxide wrought upon him more
readily than upon any other of its votaries.   " Oh, Tom ! "
he exclaims, gasping and ebullient, " Oh, Tom ! such a

gas has Davy discovered, the gaseous oxyde ! . . .
Davy has actually invented a new pleasure for which
language has no name. I am going for more this evening; it makes one strong and so happy ! so gloriously
happy ! . . . Oh, excellent air-bag ! " If Southey drew
inspiration from Davy's air-bag, could Davy do less than
lend his ear to Southey's epic ? They would stroll back
to Martin Hall—so christened because the birds who love
delicate air built under its eaves their "pendant beds,"
—and in the large sitting-room, its recesses stored with
books, or seated near the currant bushes in the garden,
the tenant of Martin Hall would read aloud of Urien and
Madoc and Cadwallon. When Davy had said good-bye,
Southey would sit long in the window open to the west,
poring on the fading glories of sunset, while about him
the dew was cool, and the swallows' tiny shrieks of glee
grew less frequent, until all was hushed and another day
was done. And sometimes he would muse how all things
that he needed for utter happiness were here,—all things
—and then would rise an ardent desire—except a child.

Martin Hall was unhappily held on no long lease ;
its owner now required possession, and the Southeys with
their household gods had reluctantly to bid it farewell.
Another trouble, and a more formidable one, at the same
time threatened. What with Annual Anthologies, Madoc
in Wales, Madoc in Aztlan, the design for a great poem on
the Deluge, for a Greek drama, for a Portuguese tragedy,
for a martyrdom play of the reign of Queen Mary, what
with reading Spanish, learning Dutch, translating and
reviewing for the booksellers, Southey had been too closely
at work. His heart began to take fits of sudden and violent pulsation ; his sleep, ordinarily as sound as a child's,
became broken and unrefreshing. Unless the disease were

thrown off by regular exercise, Beddoes assured him, it
would fasten upon him and could not be overcome. Two
years previously they had spent a summer at Burton in
Hampshire; why should they not go there again ? In June,
1799, unaccompanied by his wife, whose health seemed
also to be impaired, Southey went to seek a house.
Two cottages, convertible into one, with a garden, a fish-
pond, and a pigeon-house, promised a term of quiet and
comfort in "Southey Palace that is to be." Possession
was not to be had until Michaelmas, and part of the intervening time was very enjoyably spent in roaming
among the vales and woods, the coombes and cliffs
of Devon. It was in some measure a renewal of the
open-air delight which had been his at the Arrabida and
Cintra. "I have seen the Valley of Stones," he writes :
"Imagine a narrow vale between two ridges of hills
somewhat steep ; the southern hill turfed ; the vale which
runs from east to west covered with huge stones and
fragments of stones among the fern that fills it; the
northern ridge completely bare, excoriated of all turf and
all soil, the very bones and skeleton of the earth; rock
reclining upon rock, stone piled upon stone, a huge and
terrific mass. A palace of the Preadamite kings, a city
of the Anakim, must have appeared so shapeless and yet
so like the ruins of what had been shaped, after the waters
of the flood subsided. I ascended with some toil the
highest point; two large stones inclining on each other
formed a rude portal on the summit : here I sat down; a
little level platform about two yards long lay before me,
and then the eye fell immediately upon the sea, far, very
far below. I never felt the sublimity of solitude before."

But Southey could not rest. "I had rather leave off
eating than poetizing," he had said, and now the words

seemed coming true, for he still poetized and had almost
ceased to eat. "Yesterday I finished *Madoc*, thank God!
and thoroughly to my own satisfaction; but I have resolved
on one great, laborious and radical alteration. It was my
design to identify Madoc with Mango Capac, the legislator
of Peru: in this I have totally failed, therefore Mango
Capac is to be the hero of another poem." There is something charming in the logic of Southey's "therefore"; so
excellent an epic hero must not go to waste; but when on
the following morning he rose early it was to put on paper
the first hundred lines not of Mango Capac, but of the
Dom Daniel poem which we know as *Thalaba*. A
Mohammed to be written in hexameters was also on the
stocks; and Coleridge had promised the half of this.
Southey, who remembered a certain quarto volume on
Pantisocracy and other great unwritten works, including
the last, a Life of Lessing, by Samuel Taylor Coleridge,
knew the worth of his collaborateur's promises. However
it matters little; "the only inconvenience that his dereliction can occasion will be that I shall write the poem in
fragments and have to seam them together at last." "My
Mohammed will be what I believe the Arabian was in the
beginning of his career, sincere in enthusiasm; and it
would puzzle a casuist to distinguish between the belief of
inspiration and actual enthusiasm." A short fragment of
the *Mohammed* was actually written by Coleridge, and a
short fragment by Southey, which dating from 1799, have
an interest in connexion with the history of the English
hexameter. Last among these many projects, Southey has
made up his mind to undertake one great historical work,
the History of Portugal. This was no dream-project;
Mango Capac never descended from his father the Sun
to appear in Southey's poem; Mohammed never emerged

F

from the cavern where the spider had spread his net;
but the work which was meant to rival Gibbon's
great history was in part achieved. It is a fact more
pathetic than many others which make appeal for tears
that this most ambitious and most cherished design of
Southey's life, conceived at the age of twenty-six, and
kept constantly in view through all his days of toil, was
not yet half wrought out when forty years later the pen
dropped from his hand, and the worn-out brain could
think no more.

The deal shavings had hardly been cleared out of
the twin-cottages at Burton, when Southey was pro-
strated by a nervous fever; on recovering he moved
to Bristol, still weak, with strange pains about the heart,
and sudden seizures of the head. An entire change
of scene was obviously desirable. The sound of the
brook that ran beside his uncle's door at Cintra, the scent
of the lemon-groves, the grandeur of the Arrabida
haunted his memory; there were books and manuscripts
to be found in Portugal, which were essential in the
preparation of his great history of that country. Mr.
Hill invited him; his good friend Elmsley, an old schoolfellow, offered him a hundred pounds. From every point
of view it seemed right and prudent to go. Ailing and
unsettled as he was, he yet found strength and time to
put his hand to a good work before leaving Bristol.
Chatterton always interested Southey deeply; they had
this much at least in common, that both had often listened
to the chimes of St. Mary Redcliffe, that both were lovers
of antiquity, both were rich in store of verse and lacked
all other riches. Chatterton's sister, Mrs. Newton, and
her child were needy and neglected. It occurred to
Southey and Cottle that an edition of her brother's

poems might be published for her benefit. Subscribers came in slowly, and the plan underwent some alterations, but in the end the charitable thought bore fruit, and the sister and niece of the great unhappy boy were lifted into security and comfort. To have done something to appease the moody and indignant spirit of a dead poet was well; to have rescued from want a poor woman and her daughter was perhaps even better.

Early in April, 1800, Southey was once more on his way from Bristol by Falmouth to the Continent, accompanied by his wife, now about to be welcomed to Portugal by the fatherly uncle whose prudence she had once alarmed. The wind was adverse, and while the travellers were detained Southey strolled along the beach, caught soldier-crabs, and observed those sea-anemones which blossom anew in the verse of Thalaba. For reading on the voyage he had brought Burns, Coleridge's Poems, the Lyrical Ballads, and a poem, with "miraculous beauties," called *Gebir*, "written by God knows who." But when the ship lost sight of England, Southey with swimming head had little spirit left for wrestling with the intractable thews of Landor's early verse; he could just grunt out some crooked pun or quaint phrase in answer to inquiries as to how he did. Suddenly on the fourth morning came the announcement that a French cutter was bearing down upon them. Southey leaped to his feet, hurriedly removed his wife to a place of safety, and, musket in hand, took his post upon the quarter-deck. The smoke from the enemy's matches could be seen. She was hailed, answered in broken English, and passed on. A moment more, and the suspense was over; she was English, manned from Guernsey. "You will easily imagine," says Southey,

" that my sensations at the ending of the business were
very definable—one honest simple joy that I was in a
whole skin ! "   Two mornings more, and the sun rose
behind the Berlings ; the heights of Cintra became visible,
and nearer, the silver dust of the breakers with sea-
gulls sporting over them; a pilot's boat with puffed
and flapping sail ran out; they passed thankfully our
Lady of the Guide, and soon dropped anchor in the
Tagus.   An absence of four years had freshened every
object to Southey's sense of seeing, and now he had the
joy of viewing all familiar things as strange through so
dear a companion's eyes.

Mr. Hill was presently on board with kindly greeting ;
he had hired a tiny house for them, perched well above
the river, its little rooms cool with many doors and
windows.   Manuel the barber, brisk as Figaro, would be
their factotum, and Mrs. Southey could also see a new
maid, Maria Rosa.   Maria by-and-by came to be looked
at, in powder, straw-coloured gloves, fan, pink-ribands,
muslin petticoat, green satin sleeves ; she was " not one of
the folk who sleep on straw mattresses ;" withal she was
young and clean.   Mrs. Southey, who had liked little the
prospect of being thrown abroad upon the world, was beginning to be reconciled to Portugal ; roses and oranges,
and green peas in early May were pleasant things.   Then
the streets were an unending spectacle ; now a negro going
by with Christ in a glass case to be kissed for a petty
alms ; now some picturesque, venerable beggar ; now the
little Emperor of the Holy Ghost, strutting it from Easter
till Whitsuntide, a six-year-old mannikin with silk stock-
ings, buckles, cocked hat and sword, his gentlemen ushers
attending and his servants receiving donations on silver
salvers.   News of an assassination from time to time did

not much disturb the tranquil tenor of ordinary life.
There were old gardens to loiter in along vine-trellised
walks, or in sunshine where the grey lizards glanced and
gleamed. And eastward from the city were lovely by-
lanes amid blossoming olive-trees or market-gardens veined
by tiny aqueducts and musical with the creak of water-
wheels which told of cool refreshment. There was also
the vast public aqueduct to visit; Edith Southey, holding
her husband's hand, looked down, hardly discovering the
diminished figures below of women washing in the brook
of Alcantara. If the sultry noon in Lisbon was hard to
endure, evening made amends; then strong sea-winds
swept the narrowest alley, and rolled their current down
every avenue. And later, it was pure content to look
down upon the moonlighted river, with Almada stretching
its black isthmus into the waters that shone like midnight
snow.

Before moving to Cintra, they wished to witness the
procession of the Body of God—Southey likes the
English words as exposing "the naked nonsense of the
blasphemy"—those of St. Anthony, and the Heart of
Jesus, and the first bull-fight. Everything had grown into
one insufferable glare; the very dust was bleached, the light
was like the quivering of a furnace fire. Every man and
beast was asleep; the stone-cutter slept with his head upon
the stone; the dog slept under the very cart-wheels; the
bells alone slept not nor ceased from their importunate
clamour. At length—it was near mid June—a marvellous
cleaning of streets took place, the houses were hung with
crimson damask, soldiers came and lined the ways, windows and balconies filled with impatient watchers, not
a jewel in Lisbon but was on show. With blare of music
the procession began; first, the banners of the city and

its trades, the clumsy bearers crab-sidling along; an armed champion carrying a flag; wooden St. George held painfully on horseback; led horses, their saddles covered with rich escutcheons; all the brotherhoods, an immense train of men in red or grey cloaks; the knights of the orders superbly dressed; the whole patriarchal church in glorious robes; and then, amid a shower of rose-leaves fluttering from the windows, the Pix, and after the Pix, the Prince. On a broiling Sunday, the amusement being cool and devout, was celebrated the bull-feast. The first wound sickened Edith; Southey himself, not without an effort, looked on and saw "the death-sweat darkening the dun hide," a circumstance borne in mind for his *Thalaba*. "I am not quite sure," he writes, "that my curiosity in once going was perfectly justifiable, but the pain inflicted by the sight was expiation enough."

After this it was high time to take refuge from the sun among the lemon-groves at Cintra. Here, if ever in his life, Southey for a brief season believed that the grasshopper is wiser than the ant; a true Portuguese indolence overpowered him. "I have spent my mornings half naked in a wet room dozing upon the bed, my right hand not daring to touch my left." Such glorious indolence could only be a brief possession with Southey. More often he would wander by the streams to those spots where purple crocuses carpeted the ground, and there rest and read. Sometimes seated sideways on one of the surefooted *burros*, with a boy to beat and guide the brute, he would jog lazily on while Edith, now skilled in " asswomanship," would jog along on a brother donkey. Once and again a fog—not unwelcome—came rolling in from the ocean, one huge mass of mist, marching through the valley like a victorious army, approaching, blotting the brightness, but leaving all dank and fresh. And always the evenings were delightful, when fireflies sparkled under the trees, or in July and August as their light went out, when the grillo began his song. "I eat oranges, figs, and delicious pears—drink Colares wine, a sort of half-way excellence between port and claret—read all I can lay my hands on—dream of poem after poem, and play after play —take a siesta of two hours, and am as happy as if life were but one everlasting to-day, and that to-morrow was not to be provided for."

But Southey's second visit to Portugal was on the whole no season of repose. A week in the southern climate seemed to have restored him to health, and he assailed folio after folio in his uncle's library, rising each morning at five, "to lay in bricks for the great Pyramid of my history." The chronicles, the laws, the poetry of Portugal were among these bricks. Nor did he slacken in his ardour as a writer of verse. Six books of *Thalaba* were in his trunk in manuscript when he sailed from Falmouth; the remaining six were of a southern birth. "I am busy," he says, "in correcting *Thalaba* for the press . . . . It is a good job done, and so I have thought of another, and another, and another." As with *Joan of Arc*, so with this maturer poem the correction was a rehandling which doubled the writer's work. To draw the pen across six hundred lines did not cost him a pang. At length the manuscript was despatched to his friend Rickman, with instructions to make as good a bargain as he could for the first thousand copies. By *Joan* and the miscellaneous *Poems* of 1797, Southey had gained not far from a hundred and fifty pounds; he might fairly expect a hundred guineas for *Thalaba*. It would buy the furniture of his long-expected house. But he was concerned about the prospects of Harry, his younger brother; and now William Taylor wrote that some provincial surgeon of eminence would board and instruct the lad during four or five years for precisely a hundred guineas. " A hundred guineas ! " Southey exclaims, " well, but thank God, there is *Thalaba* ready, for which I ask this sum." " *Thalaba* finished, all my poetry," he writes, " instead of being wasted in rivulets and ditches, shall flow into the great Madoc Mississippi river." One epic poem, however, he finds too little to content him; already *The Curse of Kehama* is in his head, and another of the mythological series which never saw the light. " I have some distant view of manufacturing a Hindoo romance, wild as *Thalaba;* and a nearer one of a Persian story, of which I see the germ of vitality. I take the system of the Zendavesta for my mythology, and introduce the powers of darkness persecuting a Persian, one of the hundred and fifty sons of the great king ; an Athenian captive is a prominent character, and the whole warfare of the evil power ends in exalting a Persian prince into a citizen of Athens." From which catastrophe we may infer that Southey had still something republican about his heart.

Before quitting Portugal the Southeys, with their friend Waterhouse and a party of ladies, travelled northwards, encountering very gallantly the trials of the way ; Mafra, its convent and library, had been already visited by Southey. " Do you love reading ?" asked the friar who accompanied them, overhearing some remark about the books. " Yes." " And I," said the honest Franciscan, " love eating and drinking." At Coimbra—that central point from which radiates the history and literature of Portugal—Southey would have agreed feelingly with the good brother of the Mafra convent ; he had looked forward

to precious moments of emotion in that venerable city;
but air and exercise had given him a cruel appetite; if
truth must be told, the ducks of the monastic poultry-
yard were more to him than the precious finger of St.
Anthony. " I *did* long," he confesses, " to buy, beg, or steal
a dinner." The dinner must somehow have been secured
before he could approach in a worthy spirit that most affecting monument at Coimbra—the Fountain of Tears. " It is
the spot where Inez de Castro was accustomed to meet her
husband Pedro, and weep for him in his absence. Certainly her dwelling-house was in the adjoining garden;
and from there she was dragged, to be murdered at the
feet of the king, her father-in-law. . . . . I who have
long planned a tragedy upon the subject, stood upon my
own scene." While Southey and his companions gazed
at the fountains and their shadowing cedar-trees, the
gownsmen gathered round; the visitors were travel-
stained and bronzed by the sun ; perhaps the witty youths
cheered for the lady with the squaw tint ; whatever offence
may have been given, the ladies' protectors found them
" impudent blackguards," and with difficulty suppressed
pugilistic risings.

After an excursion southwards to Algarve, Southey made
ready for his return to England (1801). His wife desired
it, and he had attained the main objects of his sojourn
abroad. His health had never been more robust ; he had
read widely ; he had gathered large material for his History; he knew where to put his hand on this or that
which might prove needful, whenever he should return to
complete his work among the libraries of Portugal. On
arriving at Bristol, a letter from Coleridge met him. It
was dated from Greta Hall, Keswick, and after reminding
Southey that Bristol had recently lost the miraculous

young man, Davy, and adding that he, Samuel Taylor
Coleridge, had experiences, sufferings, hopes, projects to
impart, which would beguile much time, " were you on a
desert island and I your *Friday*," it went on to present
the attractions of Keswick, and in particular of Greta Hall,
in a way which could not be resisted. Taking all in all,
the beauty of the prospect, the roominess of the house,
the lowness of the rent, the unparalleled merits of the
landlord, the neighbourhood of noble libraries, it united
advantages not to be found together elsewhere. " In
short,"—the appeal wound up,—"for situation and con-
venience—and when I mention the name of Wordsworth,
for society of men of intellect—I know no place in which
you and Edith would find yourselves so well suited."

Meanwhile Drummond, an M.P. and a translator of
Persius, who was going as ambassador first to Palermo and
then to Constantinople, was on the look-out for a secretary.
The post would be obtained for Southey by his friend
Wynn, if possible ; this might lead to a consulship, why
not to the consulship at Lisbon with 1000*l.* a year ? Such
possibilities, however, could not prevent him from speedily
visiting Coleridge and Keswick. " Time and absence
make strange work with our affections," so writes Southey ;
" but mine are ever returning to rest upon you. I have
other and dear friends, but none with whom the whole of
my being is intimate. . . . . Oh ! I have yet such dreams.
Is it quite clear that you and I were not meant for some
better star, and dropped by mistake into this world of
pounds, shillings, and pence ?" So for the first time
Southey set foot in Keswick, and looked upon the lake
and the hills which were to become a portion of his being,
and which have taken him so closely, so tenderly to themselves. His first feeling was one not precisely of disap-

pointment, but certainly of remoteness from this northern
landscape ; he had not yet come out from the glow and
the noble *abandon* of the South.   " These lakes," he says,
" are like rivers ; but oh for the Mondego and the Tagus !
And these mountains beautifully indeed are they shaped
and grouped ; but oh for the grand Monchique ! and for
Cintra my paradise ! "

Time alone was needed to calm and temper his sense of
seeing, for when, leaving Mrs. Southey with her sister and
Coleridge, he visited his friend Wynn at Llangedwin, and
breathed the mountain air of his own Prince Madoc, all
the loveliness of Welsh streams and rivers sank into his
soul.   " The Dee is broad and shallow, and its dark waters
shiver into white and silver and hues of amber brown.
No mud upon the shore—no bushes—no marsh plants—
anywhere a child might stand dry-footed and dip his hand
into the water."   And again a contrasted picture : " The
mountain-side was stony and a few trees grew among its
stones ; the other side was more wooded, and had grass on
the top, and a huge waterfall thundered into the bottom,
and thundered down the bottom.   When it had nearly
passed these rocky straits, it met another stream.   The
width of water then became considerable, and twice it
formed a large black pool, to the eye absolutely stagnant,
the froth of the waters that entered there sleeping upon
the surface ; it had the deadness of enchantment ; yet was
not the pool wider than the river above it and below it,
where it foamed over and fell."   Such free delight as
Southey had among the hills of Wales came quickly to an
end.   A letter was received offering him the position of
private secretary to Mr. Corry, Chancellor of the Exche-
quer for Ireland, with a salary of four hundred pounds a
year.   Rickman was in Dublin and this was Rickman's

doing. Southey, as he was in prudence bound to do, accepted the appointment, hastened back to Keswick, bade farewell for a little while to his wife, and started for Dublin in no cheerful frame of mind.

At a later time, Southey possessed Irish friends whom he honoured and loved; he has written wise and humane words about the Irish people. But all through his career Ireland was to Southey somewhat too much that ideal country—of late to be found only in the region of humorous-pathetic melodrama—in which the business of life is carried on mainly by the agency of bulls and blunderbusses; and it required a distinct effort on his part to conceive the average Teague or Patrick otherwise than as a potato-devouring troglodyte, on occasions grotesquely amiable, but more often with the rage of Popery working in his misproportioned features. Those hours during which Southey waited for the packet were among the heaviest of his existence. After weary tackings in a baffling wind, the ship was caught into a gale, and was whirled away, fifteen miles north of Dublin to the fishing-town of Balbriggan. Then, a drive across desolate country, which would have depressed the spirits had it not been enlivened by the airs and humours of little Dr. Solomon, the unique, the omniscient, the garrulous, next after Bonaparte the most illustrious of mortals, inventor of the Cordial Balm of Gilead, and possessor of a hundred puncheons of rum. When the new private secretary arrived, the chancellor was absent; the secretary therefore set to work on rebuilding a portion of his *Madoc*. Presently Mr. Corry appeared, and there was a bow and a shake of hands; then he hurried away to London, to be followed by Southey, who going round by Keswick was there joined by his wife. From London Southey writes to Rick-

man, "The chancellor and the scribe go on in the
same way. The scribe hath made out a catalogue of all
books published since the commencement of '97 upon
finance and scarcity ; he hath also copied a paper written
by J. R. [John Rickman] containing some Irish alder-
man's hints about oak-bark ; and nothing more hath the
scribe done in his vocation. Duly he calls at the chancellor's door ; sometimes he is admitted to immediate audience ; sometimes kicketh his heels in the antechamber;
. . . . sometimes a gracious message emancipates him for
the day. Secrecy hath been enjoined him as to these
state proceedings. On three subjects he is directed to
read and research—corn-laws, finance, tythes, according to
their written order." The independent journals meanwhile had compared Corry and Southey, the two state
conspirators, to Empson and Dudley ; and delicately expressed a hope that the poet would make no false *numbers*
in his new work.

Southey, who had already worn an ass's head in one of
Gillray's caricatures, was not afflicted by the newspaper
sarcasm ; but the vacuity of such a life was intolerable,
and when it was proposed that he should become tutor
to Corry's son, he brought his mind finally to the point of
resigning "a foolish office and a good salary." His notions of competence were moderate ; the vagabondage
between the Irish and English headquarters entailed by
his office was irksome. His books were accumulating,
and there was ample work to be done among them if he
had but a quiet library of his own. Then, too, there
was another good reason for resigning. A new future was
opening for Southey. Early in the year (1802) his mother
died ; she had come to London to be with her son ;
there she had been stricken with mortal illness ; true

to her happy self-forgetful instincts, she remained calm, uncomplaining, considerate for others. "Go down, my dear ; I shall sleep presently," she had said, knowing that death was at hand. With his mother, the last friend of Southey's infancy and childhood was gone. "I calmed and curbed myself," he writes, "and forced myself to employment ; but, at night, there was no sound of feet in her bed-room, to which I had been used to listen, and in the morning it was not my first business to see her." The past was past indeed. But as the year opened, it brought a happy promise ; before summer would end, a child might be in his arms. Here were sufficient reasons for his resignation ; a library and a nursery ought, he says, to be stationary.

To Bristol husband and wife came, and there found a small furnished house. After the roar of Fleet Street, and the gathering of distinguished men—Fuseli, Flaxman, Barry, Lamb, Campbell, Bowles—there was a strangeness in the great quiet of the place. But in that quiet Southey could observe each day the growth of the pile of manuscript containing his version of *Amadis of Gaul*, for which Longman and Rees promised him a munificent sixty pounds. He toiled at his History of Portugal, finding matter of special interest in that part which was concerned with the religious orders. He received from his Lisbon collection precious boxes folio-crammed. "My dear and noble books ! Such folios of saints ! dull books enough for my patience to diet upon, till all my flock be gathered together into one fold." Sixteen volumes of Spanish poetry are lying uncut in the next room ; a folio yet untasted jogs his elbow ; two of the best and rarest chronicles coyly invite him. He had books enough in England to employ three years of active industry. And underlying all thoughts of the great Constable Nuño Alvares Pereyra, of the King D. Joaõ I., and of the Cid, deeper than the sportsman pleasure of hunting from their lair strange facts about the orders Cistercian, Franciscan, Dominican, Jesuit, there was a thought of that new-comer whom, says Southey, " I already feel disposed to call whelp and dog, and all those vocables of vituperation by which a man loves to call those he loves best."

In September, 1802, was born Southey's first child named Margaret Edith, after her mother and her dead grandmother; a flat-nosed, round-foreheaded, grey-eyed, good-humoured girl. " I call Margaret," he says in a sober mood of fatherly happiness, " by way of avoiding all commonplace phraseology of endearment, a worthy child and a most excellent character. She loves me better than any one except her mother ; her eyes are as quick as thought, she is all life and spirit, and as happy as the day is long; but that little brain of hers is never at rest, and it is painful to see how dreams disturb her." For Margery and her mother and the folios a habitation must be found. Southey inclined now towards settling in the neighbour-hood of London—now towards Norwich, where Dr. Sayers and William Taylor would welcome him, now towards Keswick; but its horrid latitude, its incessant rains ! On the whole his heart turned most fondly to Wales; and there, in one of the loveliest spots of Great Britain, in the Vale of Neath, was a house to let, by name Maes Gwyn. Southey gave his fancy the rein, and pictured himself " housed and homed" in Maes Gwyn, working steadily at the History of Portugal, and now and again glancing away from his work to have a look at Margery seated in her little great chair. But it was never to be ; a difference with the landlord brought to an end his treaty for the house, and in August the child lay dying. It was bitter to part with what had been so long desired—during seven childless years—and what had grown so dear. But Southey's heart was strong; he drew himself together, returned to his toil, now less joyous than before, and set himself to strengthen and console his wife.

Bristol was henceforth a place of mournful memories. "Edith," writes Southey, "will be nowhere so well as with her sister Coleridge. She has a little girl some six months old, and I shall try and graft her into the wound while it is yet fresh." Thus Greta Hall received its guests (September, 1803). At first the sight of little Sara Coleridge and her baby cooings caused shootings of pain on which Southey had not counted. Was the experiment of this removal to prove a failure? He still felt as if he were a feather driven by the wind. "I have no symptoms of root-striking here," he said. But he spoke, not knowing what was before him; the years of wandering were indeed over; here he had found his home.

CHAPTER IV.

THE best of life with Southey was yet to come; but in what remains there are few outstanding events to chronicle; there is nowhere any splendour of circumstance. Of some lives the virtue is distilled, as it were, into a few exquisite moments—moments of rapture, of vision, of sudden and shining achievement; all the days and years seem to exist only for the sake of such faultless moments, and it matters little whether such a life, of whose very essence it is to break the bounds of time and space, be long or short as measured by the falling of sandgrains or the creeping of a shadow. Southey's life was not one of these; its excellence was constant, uniform, perhaps somewhat too evenly distributed. He wrought in his place day after day, season after season. He submitted to the good laws of use and wont. He grew stronger, calmer, more full-fraught with stores of knowledge, richer in treasure of the heart. Time laid its hand upon him gently and unfalteringly; the bounding step became less light and swift; the ringing voice lapsed into sadder fits of silence; the raven hair changed to a snowy white; only still the indefatigable eye ran down the long folio columns, and the indefatigable hand still held the pen,—until all true life had ceased. When it has been said that Southey was appointed

G

Pye's successor in the laureateship, that he received an
honorary degree from his university, that now and again
he visited the Continent, that children were born to
him from among whom death made choice of the dearest,
and when we add that he wrote and published books, the
leading facts of Southey's life have been told. Had he
been a worse or a weaker man, we might look to find
mysteries, picturesque vices, or engaging follies ; as it is,
everything is plain, straightforward, substantial. What
makes the life of Southey eminent and singular is its unity
of purpose, its persistent devotion to a chosen object, its
simplicity, purity, loyalty, fortitude, kindliness, truth.

The river Greta, before passing under the bridge at the
end of Main Street, Keswick, winds about the little hill
on which stands Greta Hall ; its murmur may be heard
when all is still beyond the garden and orchard; to
the west it catches the evening light. "In front,"
Coleridge wrote when first inviting his friend to settle
with him, "we have a giants' camp—an encamped
army of tent-like mountains, which by an inverted
arch gives a view of another vale. On our right
the lovely vale and the wedge-shaped lake of Bassen-
thwaite ; and on our left Derwentwater and Lodore full in
view, and the fantastic mountains of Borrowdale. Behind
us the massy Skiddaw, smooth, green, high, with two
chasms and a tent-like ridge in the larger." Southey's
house belongs in a peculiar degree to his life ; in it were
stored the treasures upon which his intellect drew for
sustenance ; in it his affections found their earthly abiding-
place ; all the most mirthful, all the most mournful
recollections of Southey hang about it ; to it in every little
wandering his heart reverted like an exile's ; it was at
once his workshop and his play-ground ; and for a time,

while he endured a living death, it became his antechamber to the tomb.   The rambling tenement consisted
of two houses under one roof, the larger part being
occupied by the Coleridges and Southeys, the smaller for
a time by Mr. Jackson, their landlord.   On the ground-
floor was the parlour which served as dining-room and
general sitting-room, a pleasant chamber looking upon
the green in front; here also were Aunt Lovell's sitting-
room, and the mangling-room, in which stood ranged
in a row the long array of clogs from the greatest even
unto the least, figuring in a symbol the various stages
of human life.   The stairs to the right of the kitchen
led to a landing-place filled with bookcases; a few steps
more led to the little bedroom occupied by Mrs. Coleridge and her daughter.   " A few steps farther," writes
Sara Coleridge, whose description is here given in
abridgment, "was a little wing bedroom,—then the
study, where my uncle sat all day occupied with literary
labours and researches, but which was used as a drawing-
room for company.   Here all the tea-visiting guests were
received.   The room had three windows, a large one looking down upon the green with the wide flower-border, and
over to Keswick Lake and mountains beyond.   There
were two smaller windows looking towards the lower part
of the town seen beyond the nursery-garden.   The room
was lined with books in fine bindings; there were books
also in brackets, elegantly lettered vellum-covered volumes
lying on their sides in a heap.   The walls were hung with
pictures mostly portraits. . . . At the back of the room
was a comfortable sofa, and there were sundry tables,
beside my uncle's library table, his screen, desk, &c.
Altogether, with its internal fittings up, its noble outlook,
and something pleasing in its proportions, this was a

charming room." Hard by the study was Southey's bed-
room. We need not ramble farther through passages lined
with books, and up and down flights of stairs to Mr. Jackson's organ-room, and Mrs. Lovell's room, and Hartley's
parlour and the nurseries and the dark apple-room supposed
to be the abode of a bogle. Without, green-sward, flowers,
shrubs, strawberry-beds, fruit-trees encircled the house; to
the back, beyond the orchard a little wood stretched down
to the river side. A rough path ran along the bottom of
the wood; here on a covered seat Southey often read or
planned future work, and here his little niece loved to play
in sight of the dimpling water. "Dear Greta Hall!"
she exclaims, "and oh, that rough path beside the Greta!
How much of my childhood, of my girlhood, of my
youth were spent there!"

Southey's attachment to his mountain town and its
lakes was of no sudden growth. He came to them as one
not born under their influence; that power of hills, to
which Wordsworth owed fealty, had not brooded upon
Southey during boyhood; the rich southern meadows, the
wooded cliffs of Avon, the breezy downs had nurtured
his imagination, and to these he was still bound by pieties
of the heart. In the churchyard at Ashton, where lay his
father and his kinsfolk the beneficent cloud of mingled
love and sorrow most overshadowed his spirit. His
imagination did not soar, as did Wordsworth's, in naked
solitudes; he did not commune with a Presence imma-
nent in external nature; the world, as he viewed it, was
an admirable habitation for mankind—a habitation with
a history. Even after he had grown a mountaineer he
loved a humanized landscape, one in which the gains
of man's courage, toil, and endurance are apparent.
Flanders, where the spade has wrought its miracles

of diligence, where the slow canal-boat glides, where the *carillons* ripple from old spires, where sturdy burghers fought for freedom, and where vellum-bound quartos might be sought and found, Flanders on the whole gave Southey deeper and stronger feelings than did Switzerland. The ideal land of his dreams was always Portugal; the earthly paradise for him was Cintra with its glory of sun, and a glow even in its depths of shadow. But as the years went by, Portugal became more and more a memory, less and less a hope; and the realities of life in his home were of more worth every day. When, in 1807, it grew clear that Greta Hall was to be his life-long place of abode, Southey's heart closed upon it with a tenacious grasp. He set the plasterer and carpenter to work, he planted shrubs, he enclosed the garden, he gathered his books about him, and thought that here were materials for the industry of many years; he held in his arms children who were born in this new home; and he looked to Crosthwaite Churchyard, expecting, with quiet satisfaction, that when toil was ended he should there take his rest.

"I don't talk much about these things," Southey writes, "but these lakes and mountains give me a deep joy for which I suspect nothing elsewhere can compensate, and this is a feeling which time strengthens instead of weakening." Some of the delights of southern counties he missed; his earliest and deepest recollections were connected with flowers; both flowers and fruits were now too few; there was not a cowslip to be found near Keswick. "Here in Cumberland I miss the nightingale and the violet—the most delightful bird and the sweetest flower." But for such losses there were compensations. A pastoral land will give amiable pledges for the seasons and the

months, and will perform its engagements with a punctual
observance ; to this the mountains hardly condescend,
but they shower at their will a sudden largess of un-
imagined beauty. Southey would sally out for a constitutional at his three-mile pace, the peaked cap slightly
shadowing his eyes which were coursing over the pages of
a book held open as he walked ; he had left his study to
obtain exercise, and so to preserve health ; he was not a
laker engaged in view-hunting ; he did not affect the con-
templative mood which at the time was not and could not
be his. But when he raised his eyes, or when quickening
his three-mile to a four-mile pace he closed the book,
the beauty which lay around him liberated and soothed
his spirit. This it did unfailingly ; and it might do more,
for incalculable splendours, visionary glories, exaltations,
terrors are momentarily possible where mountain and cloud
and wind and sunshine meet. Southey, as he says, did
not talk much of these things, but they made life for him
immeasurably better than it would have been in city con-
finement ; there were spaces, vistas, an atmosphere around
his sphere of work, which lightened and relieved it.
The engagements in his study were always so numerous
and so full of interest that it needed an effort to leave
the table piled with books and papers. But a May
morning would draw him forth into the sun in spite
of himself. Once abroad, Southey had a vigorous joy in
the quickened blood, and the muscles impatient with
energy long pent up. The streams were his especial delight ; he never tired of their deep retirement, their shy
loveliness and their melody ; they could often beguile him
into an hour of idle meditation ; their beauty has in an
especial degree passed into his verse. When his sailor
brother Thomas came and settled in the Vale of New-

lands, Southey would quickly cover the ground from Keswick at his four-mile pace, and in the beck at the bottom of Tom's fields on summer days, he would plunge and re-plunge and act the river-god in the natural seats of mossy stone.   Or he would be overpowered some autumn morning by the clamour of childish voices voting a holiday by acclamation.   Their father must accompany them; it would do him good, they knew it would; they knew he did not take sufficient exercise, for they had heard him say so.   Where should the scramble be?   To Skiddaw Dod, or Causey Pike, or Watenlath, or as a compromise between their exuberant activity and his inclination for the chair and the fireside, to Walla Crag?   And there, while his young companions opened their baskets and took their noonday meal, Southey would seat himself—as Westall has drawn him—upon the bough of an ash-tree, the water flowing smooth and green at his feet, but a little higher up broken, flashing, and whitening in its fall; and there in the still autumn noon he would muse happily, placidly, not now remembering with over-keen desire the gurgling tanks and fountains of Cintra, his Paradise of early manhood.[1]

On summer days, when the visits of friends, or strangers bearing letters of introduction, compelled him to idleness, Southey's more ambitious excursions were taken.   But he was well aware that those who form acquaintance with a mountain region during a summer all blue and gold, know little of its finer power.   It is October that brings most often those days faultless, pearl-pure, of affecting influence,

> In the long year set
> Like captain jewels in the carcanet.

---

[1] For Westall's drawing, and the description of Walla Crag, see " Sir Thomas More :" Colloquy VI.

Then, as Wordsworth has said, the atmosphere seems
refined, and the sky rendered more crystalline, as the
vivifying heat of the year abates; the lights and
shadows are more delicate; the colouring is richer and
more finely harmonized; and, in this season of stillness,
the ear being unoccupied, or only gently excited, the
sense of vision becomes more susceptible of its appro-
priate enjoyments. Even December is a better month
than July for perceiving the special greatness of a moun-
tainous country. When the snow lies on the fells soft
and smooth, Grisedale Pike and Skiddaw drink in tints
at morning and evening marvellous as those seen upon
Mont Blanc or the Jungfrau for purity and richness.

"Summer," writes Southey, "is not the season for this
country. Coleridge says, and says well, that then it is
like a theatre at noon. There are no *goings on* under a
clear sky; but at other seasons there is such shifting of
shades, such islands of light, such columns and buttresses
of sunshine, as might almost make a painter burn his
brushes, as the sorcerers did their books of magic when
they saw the divinity which rested upon the apostles.
The very snow, which you would perhaps think must
monotonize the mountains, gives new varieties; it brings
out their recesses and designates all their inequalities, it
impresses a better feeling of their height, and it reflects
such tints of saffron, or fawn, or rose-colour to the evening
sun. *O Maria Santissima!* Mount Horeb with the glory
upon its summit might have been more glorious, but not
more beautiful than old Skiddaw in his winter pelisse.
I will not quarrel with frost, though the fellow has the
impudence to take me by the nose. The lake-side has
such ten thousand charms: a fleece of snow or of the hoar
frost lies on the fallen trees or large stones; the grass-

points, that just peer above the water, are powdered with
diamonds ; the ice on the margin with chains of crystal,
and such veins and wavy lines of beauty as mock all art ;
and, to crown all, Coleridge and I have found out that
stones thrown upon the lake when frozen make a noise
like singing birds, and when you whirl on it a large flake
of ice, away the shivers slide chirping and warbling like
a flight of finches." This tells of a February at Keswick ;
the following describes the *goings on* under an autumn
sky :—" The mountains on Thursday evening, before the
sun was quite down, or the moon bright, were all of one
dead-blue colour ; their rifts and rocks and swells and
scars had all disappeared—the surface was perfectly uniform, nothing but the outline distinct ; and this even
surface of dead blue, from its unnatural uniformity, made
them, though not transparent, appear transvious—as though
they were of some soft or cloudy texture through which
you could have passed. I never saw any appearance so
perfectly unreal. Sometimes a blazing sunset seems to
steep them through and through with red light ; or it is a
cloudy morning, and the sunshine slants down through a
rift in the clouds, and the pillar of light makes the spot
whereon it falls so emerald green, that it looks like a little
field of Paradise. At night you lose the mountains, and
the wind so stirs up the lake that it looks like the sea by
moonlight."

If Southey had not a companion by his side, the solitude of his ramble was unbroken ; he never had the knack
of forgathering with chance acquaintance. With intellectual and moral boldness, and with high spirits, he united a
constitutional bashfulness and reserve. His retired life,
his habits of constant study, and in later years his short-
ness of sight fell in with this infirmity. He would not

patronize his humbler neighbours ; he had a kind of imaginative jealousy on behalf of their rights as independent
persons ; and he could not be sure of straightway discovering, by any genius or instinct of good-fellowship, that
common ground whereon strangers are at home with one
another. Hence,—and Southey himself wished that it
had been otherwise,—long as he resided at Keswick
there were perhaps not twenty persons of the lower
ranks whom he knew by sight. "After slightly returning the salutation of some passer-by," says his son,
"he would again mechanically lift his cap as he heard
some well-known name in reply to his inquiries, and
look back with regret that the greeting had not been more
cordial."

If the ice were fairly broken, he found it natural
to be easy and familiar, and by those whom he employed he was regarded with affectionate reverence.
Mrs. Wilson, kind and generous creature, remained in
Greta Hall tending the children as they grew up until
she died, grieved for by the whole household. Joseph
Glover who created the scarecrow "Statues" for the
garden—male and female created he them, as the reader
may see them figured toward the close of *The Doctor*,—
Glover the artist who set up Edith's fantastic chimney-
piece ("Well, Miss Southey," cried honest Joseph, "I've
done my Devils"), was employed by Southey during
five-and-twenty years, ever since he was a 'prentice boy.
If any warm-hearted neighbour, known or unknown to him,
came forward with a demand on Southey's sympathies, he
was sure to meet a neighbourly response. When the miller,
who had never spoken to him before, invited the laureate
to rejoice with him over the pig he had killed—the finest
ever fattened—and when Southey was led to the place

where that which had ceased to be pig and was not yet
bacon, was hung up by the hind feet, he filled up the
measure of the good man's joy by hearty appreciation of
a porker's points. But Cumberland enthusiasm seldom
flames abroad with so prodigal a blaze as that of the
worthy miller's heart.

Within the charmed circle of home, Southey's temper
and manners were full of a strong and sweet hilarity; and
the home circle was in itself a considerable group of
persons. The Pantisocratic scheme of a community was
after all near finding a fulfilment, only that the Greta
ran by in place of the Susquehanna, and that Southey
took upon his own shoulders the work of the dead
Lovell, and of Coleridge, who lay in weakness and
dejection, whelmed under the tide of dreams. For some
little time Coleridge continued to reside at Keswick
an admirable companion in almost all moods of mind,
for all kinds of wisdom, and all kinds of nonsense.
When he was driven abroad in search of health, it
seemed as if a brightness were gone out of the air,
and the horizon of life had grown definite and contracted. "It is now almost ten years," Southey writes,
"since he and I first met in my rooms at Oxford,
which meeting decided the destiny of both. . . . I am
perpetually pained at thinking what he ought to be, . .
but the tidings of his death would come upon me more
like a stroke of lightning than any evil I have ever
yet endured."

Mrs. Coleridge with her children remained at Greta
Hall. That quaint little metaphysician, Hartley, now
answering to the name of Moses, now to that of
Job, the oddest of all God's creatures, was an un-
ceasing wonder and delight to his uncle—"a strange,

strange boy, 'exquisitely wild,' an utter visionary, like
the moon among thin clouds he moves in a circle of
his own making.   He alone is a light of his own.
Of all human beings I never saw one so utterly naked
of self."   When his father expressed surprise that Hartley
should take his pleasure of wheel-barrow-riding so sadly,
" The pity is "—explained little Job—" the pity is *I'se*
always thinking of my thoughts."   " 'I'm a boy of
a very religious turn,' he says ; for he always talks of
himself and examines his own character, just as if he were
speaking of another person, and as impartially.   Every
night he makes an extempore prayer aloud ; but it is
always in bed, and not till he is comfortable there and got
into the mood.   When he is ready, he touches Mrs. Wilson,
who sleeps with him, and says, ' Now listen ! ' and off he
sets like a preacher."   Younger than Hartley was Derwent
Coleridge, a fair broad-chested boy, with merry eye
and roguish lips, now grown out of that yellow frock
in which he had earned his name of Stumpy Canary.
Sara Coleridge, when her uncle came to Keswick after
the death of his own Margery, was a little grand-lama
at that worshipful age of seven months.   A fall into
the Greta a year and a half later, helped to change her
to the delicate creature, whose large blue eyes would look
up timidly from under her lace border and mufflings
of muslin.   No feeling towards their father save a
reverent loyalty did the Coleridge children ever learn
under Southey's roof.   But when the pale-faced wanderer
returned from Italy, he surprised and froze his daughter
by a sudden revelation of that jealousy which is the fond
injustice of an unsatisfied heart, and which a child who
has freely given and taken love finds it hard to comprehend.   "I think my dear father," writes Sara Coleridge,

"was anxious that I should learn to love him and the Wordsworths and their children, and not cling so exclusively to my mother and all around me at home." Love him and revere his memory she did ; to Wordsworth she was conscious of owing more than to any other teacher or inspirer in matters of the intellect and imagination. But in matters of the heart and conscience the daily life of Southey was the book in which she read ; he was, she would emphatically declare, " upon the whole the best man she had ever known."

But the nepotism of the most "nepotious" uncle is not a perfect substitute for fatherhood with its hopes and fears. May-morning of the year 1804, saw "an Edithling very, very ugly, with no more beauty than a young dodo," nestling by Edith Southey's side. A trembling thankfulness possessed the little one's father ; but when the Arctic weather changed suddenly to days of genial sunshine, and groves and gardens burst into living greenery, and rang with song, his heart was caught into the general joy. Southey was not without a presentiment that his young dodo would improve. Soon her premature activity of eye and spirits troubled him, and he tried while cherishing her to put a guard upon his heart. " I did not mean to trust my affections again on so frail a foundation,—and yet the young one takes me from my desk and makes me talk nonsense as fluently as you perhaps can imagine." When Sara Coleridge,—not yet five years old, but already, as she half believed, promised in marriage to Mr. De Quincey,—returned after a short absence to Greta Hall, she saw her baby cousin, sixteen months younger, and therefore not yet marriageable, grown into a little girl very fair, with thick golden hair, and round rosy cheeks. Edith Southey inherited something of her father's looks,

and of his swift intelligence ; with her growing beauty
of face and limbs a growing excellence of inward nature
kept pace. At twenty she was the "elegant cygnet" of
Amelia Opie's album verses,

> 'Twas pleasant to meet
> And see thee famed Swan of the Derwent's fair tide
> With that elegant cygnet that floats by thy side,

a compliment her father mischievously would not let her
Elegancy forget.   Those who would know her in the loveliness of youthful womanhood may turn to Wordsworth's
poem *The Triad*, where she appears first of the three
"sister nymphs" of Keswick and Rydal ; or, Hartley
Coleridge's exquisite sonnet, *To a lofty beauty from her
poor kinsman :—*

> Methinks thy scornful mood,
> And bearing high of stately womanhood,—
> Thy brow where Beauty sits to tyrannize
> O'er humble love, had made me sadly fear thee :
> For never sure was seen a royal bride,
> Whose gentleness gave grace to so much pride—
> My very thoughts would tremble to be near thee,
> But when I see thee by thy father's side
> Old times unqueen thee, and old loves endear thee.

But it is best of all to remember Southey's daughter in
connexion with one letter of her father's.   In 1805 he
visited Scotland alone ; he had looked forward to carrying
on the most cherished purpose of his life—the History of
Portugal—among the libraries of Lisbon.   But it would
be difficult to induce Mrs. Southey to travel with the
Edithling.   Could he go alone ?   The short absence in
Scotland served to test his heart, and so to make his future
clear :—

  "I need not tell you, my own dear Edith, not to read my
letters aloud till you have first of all seen what is written only

for yourself.   What I have now to say to you is, that having been eight days from home, with as little discomfort, and as little reason for discomfort, as a man can reasonably expect, I have yet felt so little comfortable, so great sense of solitariness and so many homeward yearnings, that certainly I will not go to Lisbon without you ; a resolution which, if your feelings be at all like mine, will not displease you. If, on mature consideration, you think the inconvenience of a voyage more than you ought to submit to, I must be content to stay in England, as on my part it certainly is not worth while to sacrifice a year's happiness ; for though not unhappy (my mind is too active and too well disciplined to yield to any such criminal weakness), still without you I am not happy.   But for your sake as well as my own, and for little Edith's sake I will not consent to any separation ; the growth of a year's love between her and me, if it please God that she should live, is a thing too delightful in itself, and too valuable in its consequences, both to her and me, to be given up for any light inconvenience either on your part or mine.   An absence of a year would make her effectually forget me. . . . . But of these things we will talk at leisure ; only dear, dear Edith, we must not part."

Such wisdom of the heart was justified ; the year of growing love bore precious fruit.   When Edith May was ten years old her father dedicated to her, in verses laden with a father's tenderest thoughts and feelings, his *Tale of Paraguay*.   He recalls the day of her birth, the preceding sorrow for his first child whose infant features have faded from him like a passing cloud ; the gladness of that singing month of May ; the seasons that followed during which he observed the dawning of the divine light in her eyes ; the playful guiles by which he won from her repeated kisses ; to him these ten years seem like yesterday ; but to her they have brought discourse of reason, with the sense of time and change :—

And I have seen thine eyes suffused in grief
When I have said that with autumnal grey

The touch of eld hath mark'd thy father's head ;
That even the longest day of life is brief,
And mine is falling fast into the yellow leaf.

Other children followed, until a happy stir of life filled
the house. Emma, the quietest of infants, whose voice
was seldom heard, and whose dark-grey eyes too seldom
shone in her father's study, slipped quietly out of the
world after a hand's-breadth of existence ; but to Southey
she was no more really lost than the buried brother
and sister were to the cottage girl of Wordsworth's
We are seven. " I have five children," he says in 1809 ;
"three of them at home, and two under my mother's
care in heaven."   Of all the most radiantly beautiful
was Isabel ; the most passionately loved was Herbert.
" My other two are the most perfect contrast you ever
saw. Bertha, whom I call Queen Henry the Eighth,
from her likeness to King Bluebeard, grows like Jonah's
gourd, and is the very picture of robust health ; and little
Kate hardly seems to grow at all, though perfectly well,—
she is round as a mushroom-button. Bertha, the bluff
queen, is just as grave as Kate is garrulous ; they are
inseparable play-fellows, and go about the house hand in
hand."

Among the inmates of Greta Hall, to overlook Lord
Nelson and Bona Marietta, with their numerous successors,
would be a grave delinquency.   To be a cat was to be a
privileged member of the little republic to which Southey
gave laws.   Among the fragments at the end of *The
Doctor* will be found a Chronicle History of the Cattery
of Cat's Eden, and some of Southey's frolic letters are
written as if his whole business in life were that of
secretary for feline affairs in Greta Hall.   A house, he
declared, is never perfectly furnished for enjoyment unless

there is in it a child rising three years old and a kitten rising six weeks; "kitten is in the animal world what the rosebud is in the garden." Lord Nelson, an ugly specimen of the streaked-carroty or Judas-coloured kind, yet withal a good cat, affectionate, vigilant, and brave, was succeeded by Madame Bianchi, a beautiful and singular creature, white with a fine tabby tail; "her wild eyes were bright and green as the Duchess de Cadaval's emerald necklace." She fled away with her niece Pulcheria on the day when good old Mrs. Wilson died; nor could any allurements induce the pair to domesticate themselves again. For some time a cloud of doom seemed to hang over Cat's Eden. Ovid and Virgil, Othello the Moor, and Pope Joan perished miserably. At last Fortune, as if to make amends for her unkindness, sent to Greta Hall almost together the never-to-be-enough-praised Rumpelstilzchen (afterwards raised for services against rats to be His Serene Highness the Archduke Rumpelstilzchen), and the equally-to-be-praised Hurlyburlybuss. With whom too soon we must close the catalogue.

The revenue to maintain this household was in the main won by Southey's pen. "It is a difficult as well as a delicate task," he wrote in the *Quarterly Review*, "to advise a youth of ardent mind and aspiring thoughts in the choice of a profession; but a wise man will have no hesitation in exhorting him to choose anything rather than literature. Better that he should seek his fortune before the mast, or with a musket on his shoulder and a knapsack on his back, better that he should follow the plough, or work at the loom or the lathe, or sweat over the anvil, than trust to literature as the only means of his support." Southey's own bent towards literature was too strong to be altered. But, while he accepted loyally the burdens

H

of his profession as a man of letters, he knew how stout a
back is needed to bear them month after month and year
after year.   Absolutely dependent on his pen he was
at no time.   His generous friend Wynn, upon coming
of age, allowed him annually 160*l.*, until in 1807 he was
able to procure for Southey a Government pension for
literary services amounting, clear of taxes, to nearly the
same sum.   Southey had as truly as any man the pride
of independence, but he had none of its vanity ; there was
no humiliation in accepting a service from one whom
friendship had made as close as a brother ; men, he says,
are as much better for the good offices which they receive
as for those they bestow ; and his own was no niggard
hand.   Knowing both to give and to take, with him the
remembrance that he owed much to others was among the
precious possessions of life which bind us to our kind
with bonds of sonship not of slavery.   Of the many kind-
nesses which he received he never forgot one.   "Had it
not been for your aid," he writes to Wynn, forty years
after their first meeting in Dean's Yard, "I should have
been irretrievably wrecked when I ran upon the shoals,
with all sail set, in the very outset of my voyage."   And to
another good old friend who from his own modest station
applauded while Southey ran forward in the race : "Do
you suppose, Cottle, that I have forgotten those true and
most essential acts of friendship which you showed me
when I stood most in need of them ?   Your house was my
house when I had no other.   The very money with which
I bought my wedding-ring and paid my marriage-fees, was
supplied by you.   It was with your sisters I left Edith
during my six months' absence, and for the six months
after my return it was from you that I received, week by
week, the little on which we lived, till I was enabled to

live by other means. It is not the settling of a cash account that can cancel obligations like these. You are in
the habit of preserving your letters, and if you were not,
I would entreat you to preserve *this* that it might be seen
hereafter. . . . . My head throbs and my eyes burn with
these recollections. Good night ! my dear old friend and
benefactor."

Anxiety about his worldly fortunes never cost Southey
a sleepless night. His disposition was always hopeful ; relying on Providence, he says, I could rely upon
myself. When he had little, he lived upon little,
never spending when it was necessary to spare, and his
means grew with his expenses. Business habits he
had none ; never in his life did he cast up an account ;
but in a general way he knew that money comes by
honest toil and grows by diligent husbandry. Upon
Mrs. Southey, who had an eye to all the household out-
goings, the cares of this life fell more heavily. Sara
Coleridge calls to mind her aunt as she moved about
Greta Hall intent on house affairs, "with her fine figure
and quietly commanding air." Alas ! under this gracious
dignity of manner the wear and tear of life were doing
their work surely. Still, it was honest wear and tear.
" I never knew her to do an unkind act," says Southey,
"nor say an unkind word ; " but when stroke followed
upon stroke of sorrow, they found her without that elastic
temper which rises and recovers itself. Until the saddest
of afflictions made her helpless, everything was left to her
management and was managed so quietly and well, that except in times of sickness and bereavement, " I had," writes
her husband, "literally no cares." Thus free from harass
Southey toiled in his library ; he toiled not for bread
alone, but also for freedom. There were great designs

before him which, he was well aware, if ever realized
would make but a poor return to the household coffer. To
gain time and a vantage-ground for these he was content
to yield much of his strength to work of temporary
value, always contriving however to strike a mean in this
journeyman service between what was most and least
akin to his proper pursuits. When a parcel of books
arrived from the Annual Review, he groaned in spirit
over the sacrifice of time; but patience! it is after all
better, he would reflect, than pleading in a court of law ;
better than being called up at midnight to a patient;
better than calculating profit and loss at a counter; better in short than anything but independence. "I am
a quiet, patient, easy-going hack of the mule breed,"
—he writes to Grosvenor Bedford,—"regular as clock-
work in my pace, sure-footed, bearing the burden which
is laid on me, and only obstinate in choosing my own path.
If Gifford could see me by this fireside where, like
Nicodemus, one candle suffices me in a large room, he
would see a man in a coat 'still more threadbare than his
own,' when he wrote his 'Imitation,' working hard and
getting little—a bare maintenance, and hardly that ;
writing poems and history for posterity with his whole
heart and soul ; one daily progressive in learning, not so
learned as he is poor, not so poor as proud ; not so proud
as happy. Grosvenor, there is not a lighter-hearted nor a
happier man upon the face of this wide world." When
these words were written, Herbert stood by his father's
side ; it was sweet to work that his boy might have his
play-time glad and free.

The public estimate of Southey's works as expressed in
pounds, shillings, and pence was lowest where he held
that it ought to have been highest. For the *History of*

Brazil, a work of stupendous toil, which no one in England could have produced save Southey himself, he had not received after eight years, as much as for a single article in the Quarterly Review. *Madoc*, the pillar, as he supposed, on which his poetical fame was to rest, *Madoc*, which he dismissed with an awed feeling as if in it he were parting with a great fragment of his life, brought its author after twelve months' sales the sum of three pounds, seventeen shillings and one penny. On the other hand, for his *Naval Biography*, which interested him less than most of his works, and which was undertaken after hesitation, he was promised five hundred guineas a volume. Notwithstanding his unwearied exertions, his modest scale of expenditure, and his profitable connexion with the *Quarterly Review*—for an important article he would receive one hundred pounds—he never had a year's income in advance until that year late in his life in which Sir Robert Peel offered him a baronetcy. In 1818, the lucky payment of a bad debt enabled him to buy three hundred pounds in the Three-per-cents. " I have 100*l.* already there," he writes " and shall then be worth 12*l.* per annum." By 1821 this sum had grown to 625*l.*, the gatherings of half a life-time. In that year his friend John May, whose acquaintance he had made in Portugal, and to whose kindness he was a debtor, suffered the loss of his fortune. As soon as Southey had heard the state of affairs, his decision was formed. " By this post," he tells his friend, " I write to Bedford, desiring that he will transfer to you 625*l.* in the Three-per-cents. I wish it was more and that I had more at my command in any way. I shall in the spring, if I am paid for the first volume of my History as soon as it is finished. One hundred I should, at all events, have sent you then. It shall be as much more as I receive." And he goes on in cheery words to invite John May to break away from business and come to Keswick, there to lay in "a pleasant store of recollections which in all moods of mind are wholesome." One rejoices that Southey, poor of worldly goods, knew the happiness of being so simply and nobly generous.

Blue and white china, mediæval ivories, engravings by the Little Masters, Chippendale cabinets, did not excite pining desire in Southey's breast; yet in one direction he indulged the passion of a collector. If with respect to any of "the things independent of the will," he showed a want of moderation unworthy of his discipleship to Epictetus, it was assuredly with respect to books. Before he possessed a fixed home he was already moored to his folios; and when once he was fairly settled at Keswick, many a time the carriers on the London road found their lading the larger by a weighty packet on its way to Greta Hall. Never did he run north or south for a holiday, but the inevitable parcel preceded or followed his return. Never did he cross to the Continent but a bulkier bale arrived in its own good time enclosing precious things. His morality, in all else void of offence, here yielded to the seducer. It is thought that Southey was in the main honest; but if Dirk Hatteraick had run ashore a hundredweight of the Acta Sanctorum duty-free, the king's laureate was not the man to set the sharks upon him, and it is to be feared that the pattern of probity, the virtuous Southey himself, might in such circumstances be found, under cover of night, lugging his prize landwards from its retreat beneath the rocks. Unquestionably at one time certain parcels from Portugal—only of such a size as could be carried under the

arm—were silently brought ashore to the defrauding of
the revenue, and somehow found their way by-and-by to
Greta Hall. "We maintain a trade," says the Governor
of the Strangers' House in Bacon's philosophical romance,
"not for gold, silver or jewels, nor for silks, nor for spices,
nor any other commodity of matter, but only for God's
first creature, which was *light*." Such too was Southey's
trade, and he held that God's first creature is free to travel
unchallenged by revenue-cutter.

"Why, Montesinos," asks the ghostly Sir Thomas More
in one of Southey's *Colloquies*, "with these books and
the delight you take in their constant society, what
have you to covet or desire?" "Nothing," is the answer,
" . . . . except more books." When Southey, in 1805,
went to see Walter Scott, it occurred to him in Edinburgh that having had neither new coat nor hat since little
Edith was born he must surely be in want of both, and
here, in the metropolis of the North, was an opportunity
of arraying himself to his desire. "Howbeit," he says, "on
considering the really respectable appearance which my
old ones made for a traveller,—and considering, moreover,
that as learning was better than house or land, it certainly must be much better than fine clothes—I laid out
all my money in books, and came home to wear out
my old wardrobe in the winter." De Quincey called
Southey's library his wife, and in a certain sense it was
wife and mistress and mother to him. The presence and
enjoying of his books was not the sole delight they
afforded; their was also the pursuit, the surprisal, the
love-making or wooing. And at last in his hours of weakness, once more a little child, he would walk slowly
round his library, looking at his cherished volumes, taking
them down mechanically, and when he could no longer

read, pressing them to his lips. In happier days the bookstalls of London knew the tall figure, the rapid stride,
the quick-seeking eye, the eager fingers. Lisbon, Paris,
Milan, Amsterdam contributed to the rich confusion that,
from time to time, burdened the floors of library and bed-
rooms and passages in Greta Hall. Above all he was
remembered at Brussels by that best of bookmen, Ver·
beyst. What mattered it that Verbeyst was a sloven, now
receiving his clients with gaping shirt and now with
stockingless feet ; did he not duly honour letters, and had
he not 300,000 volumes from which to choose ? If in a
moment of prudential weakness one failed to carry off
such a treasure as the Monumenta Boica, or Colgar's Irish
Saints, there was a chance that in Verbeyst's vast storehouse the volume might lurk for a year or two. And Verbeyst loved his books ; only less than he loved his handsome good-natured wife, who for a liberal customer would
fetch the bread and burgundy. Henry Taylor dwelt in
Robert Southey's heart of hearts ; but let not Henry Taylor
treasonably hint that Verbeyst, the prince of booksellers,
had not a prince's politeness of punctuality. If sundry
books promised had not arrived, it was because they were
not easily procured ; moreover, the good-natured wife had
died—*bien des malheurs*, and Verbeyst's heart was fallen
into a lethargy. "Think ill of our fathers which are in
the Row, think ill of John Murray, think ill of Colburn,
think ill of the whole race of bibliopoles, except Verbeyst,
who is always to be thought of with liking and respect."
And when the bill of lading, coming slow but sure, announced that saints and chroniclers and poets were on
their way, "by this day month," wrote Southey, "they
will probably be here ; then shall I be happier than if his
Majesty King George the Fourth were to give orders that

I should be clothed in purple, and sleep upon gold, and
have a chain upon my neck, and sit next him because
of my wisdom, and be called his cousin."

Thus the four thousand volumes, which lay piled about
the library when Southey first gathered his possessions together, grew and grew, year after year until the grand total
mounted up to eight, to ten, to fourteen thousand. Now Kirke
White's brother Neville sends him a gift of Sir William
Jones's works, thirteen volumes, in binding of bewildering
loveliness. Now Landor ships from some Italian port a chest
containing treasures of less dubious value than the Raf-
faelles and Leonardos with which he liberally supplied his
art-loving friends.   Oh, the joy of opening such a chest ;
of discovering the glorious folios ; of glancing with the
shy amorousness of first desire at title-page and colophon ;
of growing familiarity ; of tracing out the history suggested
by book-plate or autograph ; of finding a lover's excuses
for cropped margin, or water-stain, or worm-hole.   Then
the calmer happiness of arranging his favourites on new
shelves ; of taking them down again after supper in
the season of meditation and currant-rum ; and of won-
dering for which among his father's books Herbert will
care most when all of them shall be his own.   " It
would please you," Southey writes to his old comrade,
Bedford, " to see such a display of literary wealth, which
is at once the pride of my eye, and the joy of my heart, and
the food of my mind ; indeed, more than metaphorically,
meat, drink and clothes for me and mine. I verily believe
that no one in my station was ever so rich before, and I
am very sure that no one in any station had ever a more
thorough enjoyment of riches of any kind or in any way."

Southey's Spanish and Portuguese collection—if Heber's
great library be set aside—was probably the most remark-

able gathering of such books in the possession of any
private person in this country. It included several manuscripts, some of which were displayed with due distinction
upon brackets. Books in white and gold—vellum or parchment bound, with gilt lettering in the old English type
which Southey loved—were arranged in effective positions
pyramid-wise. Southey himself had learned the mystery
of book-binding, and from him his daughters acquired
that art ; the ragged volumes were decently clothed in
coloured cotton prints ; these, presenting a strange patch-
work of colours, quite filled one room which was known
as the Cottonian Library. " Paul," a book-room on
the ground floor, had been so called because " Peter "
the organ-room was robbed to fit it with books. " Paul
is a great comfort to us, and being dressed up with
Peter's property, makes a most respectable appearance, and
receives that attention which is generally shown to the
youngest child. The study has not actually been Petered
on Paul's account, but there has been an exchange nego-
tiated which we think is for their mutual advantage.
Twenty gilt volumes, from under the ' Beauties of England and Wales,' have been marched down-stairs rank and
file, and their place supplied by the long set of Lope de
Vega with green backs."

   Southey's books, as he assures his ghostly monitor in the
Colloquies, were not drawn up on his shelves for display,
however much the pride of the eye might be gratified in
beholding them ; they were on actual service. Generations
might pass away before some of them would again find a
reader; in their mountain home they were prized and known
as perhaps they never had been known before. Not a few
of the volumes had been cast up from the wreck of family
or convent libraries during the Revolution. " Yonder Acta

Sanctorum belonged to the Capuchines at Ghent. This book of St. Bridget's Revelations, in which not only all the initial letters are illuminated, but every capital throughout the volume was coloured, came from the Carmelite Nunnery at Bruges. . Here are books from Colbert's library ; here others from the Lamoignon one. . Yonder Chronicle History of King D. Manoel, by Damiam de Goes, and yonder General History of Spain, by Esteban de Garibay, are signed by their respective authors. . . This Copy of Casaubon's Epistles was sent to me from Florence by Walter Landor. He had perused it carefully, and to that perusal we are indebted for one of the most pleasing of his Conversations. . Here is a book with which Lauderdale amused himself, when Cromwell kept him in prison in Windsor Castle. . Here I possess these gathered treasures of time, the harvest of many generations, laid up in my garners : and when I go to the window there is the lake, and the circle of the mountains, and the illimitable sky."

Not a few of his books were dead, and to live among these was like living among the tombs ; " Behold, this also is vanity," Southey makes confession. But when Sir Thomas questions, " Has it proved to you ' vexation of spirit ' also ? " the Cumberland mountain-dweller breaks forth : " Oh no ! for never can any man's life have been past more in accord with his own inclinations nor more answerably to his desires. Excepting that peace, which, through God's infinite mercy, is derived from a higher source, it is to literature, humanly speaking, that I am beholden, not only for the means of subsistence, but for every blessing which I enjoy ; health of mind and activity of mind, contentment, cheerfulness, continual employment and therefore continual pleasure. *Suavissima*

vita indies sentire se fieri meliorem; and this as Bacon has
said, and Clarendon repeated, is the benefit that a studious
man enjoys in retirement." Such a grave gladness under-
lay all Southey's frolic moods, and in union with a clear-
sighted acceptance of the conditions of human happiness,—
its inevitable shocks, its transitory nature as far as it belongs to man's life on earth—made up part of his habitual
temper.

Southey coursed from page to page with a greyhound's
speed ; a tiny *s* pencilled in the margin served to indi-
cate what might be required for future use. Neatness
he had learnt from Miss Tyler long ago ; and by experience he acquired his method. On a slip of paper
which served as marker he would note the pages to
which he needed to return. In the course of a few
hours he had classified and arranged everything in a
book which it was likely he would ever want. A reference
to the less important passages sufficed ; those of special
interest were transcribed by his wife, or one of his
daughters, or more frequently by Southey himself ; finally,
these transcripts were brought together in packets under
such headings as would make it easy to discover any
portion of their contents.

Such was his ordinary manner of eviscerating an author,
but it was otherwise with the writers of his affection. On
some—such as Jackson and Jeremy Taylor—" he *fed*,"
as he expressed it, " slowly and carefully, dwelling on
the page, and taking in its contents, deeply and deli-
berately, like an epicure with his wine 'searching the
subtle flavour.'" Such chosen writers remained for all
times and seasons faithful and cherished friends :—

> With them I take delight in weal,
> And seek relief in woe ;

> And while I understand and feel
>   How much to them I owe,
> My cheeks have often been bedewed
>   With tears of thankful gratitude.

" If I were confined to a score of English books," says
Southey, " Sir Thomas Browne would, I think, be one of
them ; nay probably it would be one if the selection were
cut down to twelve. My library, if reduced to those
bounds, would consist of Shakspeare, Chaucer, Spenser,
and Milton ; Jackson, Jeremy Taylor, and South ; Isaac
Walton, Sidney's Arcadia, Fuller's Church History, and
Sir Thomas Browne ; and what a wealthy and well-stored
mind would that man have, what an inexhaustible reser-
voir, what a Bank of England to draw upon for profitable
thoughts and delightful associations, who should have fed
upon them." It must have gone hard with Southey in
making out this list, to exclude Clarendon, and doubtless
if the choice were not limited to books written in English,
the Utopia would have urged its claim to admission. With
less difficulty he could skip the whole of the eighteenth
century. From *Samson Agonistes* to *The Task* there was
no English poem which held a foremost place in his esteem.
Berkeley and Butler he valued highly ; but Robert South
seemed to him the last of the race of the giants. An
ancestral connection with Locke was not a source of pride
to Southey ; he respected neither the philosopher's politics
nor his metaphysics ; still it is pleasant, he says, to hear
of somebody between oneself and Adam who has left a
name.

Four volumes of what are called Southey's *Commonplace Books* have been published, containing some three
thousand double-column pages ; and these are but a selection from the total mass of his transcripts. It is impossible

to give a notion of a miscellany drawn from so wide-ranging a survey of poetry, biography, history, travels, topography, divinity, not in English alone, but also in Latin, French, Italian, Spanish, Portuguese. Yet certain main lines can be traced which give some meaning to this huge accumulation. It is easy to perceive that the collector wrought under an historical bias, and that social, literary, and ecclesiastical history were the directions in which the historical tendency found its play. Such work of transcribing, though it did not rest Southey's hand, was a relief to his mind after the excitement of composition, and some of it may pass for a kind of busy idleness ; but most of his transcripts were made with a definite purpose—that of furnishing materials for work either actually accomplished, or still in prospect, when at last the brain grew dull and the fingers slack. "I am for ever making collections," he writes, "and storing up materials which may not come into use till the Greek Calends. And this I have been doing for five and twenty years ! It is true that I draw daily upon my hoards, and should be poor without them ; but in prudence I ought now to be working up those materials rather than adding to so much dead stock." When Ticknor visited him in 1819, Southey opened for the young American his great bundles of manuscript materials for the History of Portugal, and the History of the Portuguese East Indies. Southey had charmed him by the kindness of his reception, by the air of culture and of goodness in his home, by his talk bright and eager, " for the quickness of his mind expresses itself in the fluency of his utterance, and yet he is ready upon almost any subject that can be proposed to him from the extent of his knowledge." And now when Ticknor saw spread before him the evidence of such unexampled industry, a kind of bewilderment took possession of him. " Southey," he writes in his diary, "is certainly an extraordinary man, one of those whose characters I find it difficult to comprehend, because I hardly know how such elements can be brought together, such rapidity of mind with such patient labour and wearisome exactness, so mild a disposition with so much nervous excitability, and a poetical talent so elevated with such an immense mass of minute dull learning."

If Ticknor had been told that this was due to Epictetus, it might have puzzled him still more; but it is certain that only through the strenuous appliance of will to the formation of character could Southey have grown to be what he was. He had early been possessed by the belief that he must not permit himself to become the slave or the victim of sensibility, but that in the little world of man there are two powers ruling by a Divine right—reason and conscience, in loyal obedience to which lies our highest freedom. Then, too, the circumstances of his life prompted him to self-mastery and self-management. That he should every day overtake a vast amount of work was not left to his choosing or declining—it was a matter of necessity ; to accomplish this he must get all possible advantage out of his rapidity of intellect and his energy of feeling, and at the same time he must never put an injurious strain on these. It would not do for Southey to burn away to-day in some white flame of excitement the nerve which he needed for use to-morrow. He could not afford to pass a sleepless night. If his face glowed or his brain throbbed, it was a warning that he had gone far enough. His very susceptibility to nervous excitement rendered caution the more requisite. William Taylor had compared him to the mimosa. Hazlitt remembered him with a quivering lip, a hectic flush upon his cheek, a roving fire in his eye, a falcon glance, a look at once aspiring and dejected. Crabb Robinson found in him a likeness to Shelley. Humphrey Davy had proved the fineness of his sensibility by that odd neurometer the nitrous oxide. " The truth is," writes Southey, " that though some persons, whose knowledge of me is scarcely skin-deep, suppose I have no nerves, because I have great self-control as far as regards the surface, if it were not for great self-management, and what may be called a strict intellectual regimen, I should very soon be in a deplorable state of what is called nervous disease, and this would have been the case any time during the last twenty years." And again : " A man had better break a bone, or even lose a limb, than shake his nervous system. I, who never talk about my nerves (and am supposed to have none by persons who see as far into me as they do into a stone wall) know this." Southey could not afford to play away his health at hazard, and then win it back in the lounge of some foreign watering-place. His plan, on the contrary, was to keep it and to think about it as little as possible. A single prescription sufficed for a life-time—*In labore quies.* " I think I may lay claim," he says, " to the praise of self-management both in body and mind without paying too much attention to either—exercising a diseased watchfulness or playing any tricks with either." It would not have been difficult for Southey, with such a temperament as his, to have wrecked himself at the outset of his career. With beautiful foiled lives of young men Southey had a peculiar sympathy. But the gods sometimes give white hairs as an aureole to their favoured ones. Perhaps on the whole for him it was not only more prudent but also more chivalrous to study to be quiet; to create a home for those who looked to him for security;

to guard the happiness of tender women; to make smooth
ways for the feet of little children; to hold hands in old
age with the friends of his youth; to store his mind with
treasures of knowledge; to strengthen and chasten his
own heart; to grow yearly in love for his country and her
venerable heritage of manners, virtue, laws; to add to
her literature the outcome of an adult intellect and
character; and having fought a strenuous and skilful fight,
to fall as one whose sword an untimely stroke has shattered
in his hand.

I

CHAPTER V.

THE texture of Southey's life was so uniform, the round from morning till night repeated itself with so much regularity, that one day may stand as representative of a thousand. We possess his record of how the waking hours went by when he was about thirty years old, and a similar record written when he was twice that age. His surroundings had changed in the meantime, and he himself had changed; the great bare room which he used from the first as a study, fresh-plastered in 1804, with the trowel lines on the ceiling pierced by the flaws of winter, containing two chairs and a little table,—" God help me," he exclaims, "I look in it like a cock-robin in a church" —this room had received long before 1834, its lining of comely books, its white and gold pyramids, its brackets, its cherished portraits. The occupant of the study had the same spare frame, the same aspect of lightness and of strength, the same full eyebrows shadowing the dark brown eyes, the same variously expressive muscular mouth; the youthful wildness in his countenance had given place to a thoughtful expression, and the abundant hair still clustering over his great brow was snowy white. Whatever had changed, his habits—though never his tyrants—remained, with some variations in detail, the same. "My actions," he writes to a friend not very long after his arrival in Keswick, "are as regular as those of St. Dunstan's quarter-boys. Three pages of history after breakfast (equivalent to five in small quarto printing) ; then to transcribe and copy for the press, or to make my selections and biographies, or what else suits my humour till dinner-time ; from dinner to tea I read, write letters, see the newspaper, and very often indulge in a siesta—for sleep agrees with me. . . . After tea I go to poetry and correct and re-write and copy till I am tired, and then turn to anything else till supper ; and this is my life,—which if it be not a very merry one, is yet as happy as heart could wish." " See how the day is disposed of !" begins the later record, "I get out of bed as the clock strikes six, and shut the house-door after me as it strikes seven.[1]   After two hours with Davies, home to breakfast, after which Cuthbert engages me till about half-past ten, and when the post brings no letters that either interest or trouble me (for of the latter I have many), by eleven I have done with the newspaper, and can then set about what is properly the business of the day.   But letters are often to be written, and I am liable to frequent interruptions ; so that there are not many mornings in which I can command from two to three unbroken hours at the desk.   At two I take my daily walk, be the weather what it may, and when the weather permits, with a book in my hand ; dinner at four, read about half an hour ; then take to the sofa with a different book, and after a few pages get my soundest sleep, till summoned to tea at six.   My best time during the winter is by candle-light ; twilight inter-

[1] I.e. to go to Davies' lodgings; Davies, Dr. Bell's Secretary, was engaged in arranging a vast accumulation of papers with a view to forwarding Southey in his *Life of Bell*.

feres with it a little; and in the season of company I can never count upon an evening's work. Supper at half-past nine, after which I read an hour, and then to bed. The greatest part of my miscellaneous work is done in the odds and ends of time."

It was part of Southey's regimen to carry on several works at once; this he found to be economy of time, and he believed it necessary for the preservation of his health. Whenever one object entirely occupied his attention, it haunted him, oppressed him, troubled his dreams. The remedy was simple—to do one thing in the morning, another in the evening. To lay down poetry and presently to attack history seems feasible and no ill policy for one who is forced to take all he can out of himself; but Southey would turn from one poetical theme to another, and could day by day advance with a pair of epics. This was a source of unfailing wonder to Landor. "When I write a poem," he says, "my heart and all my feelings are upon it. . . . High poems will not admit flirtation." Little by little was Southey's way, and so he got on with many things. "Last night," he writes to Bedford, "I began the Preface [to "Specimens of English Poets"]—huzza! And now, Grosvenor, let me tell you what I have to do. I am writing— 1. The History of Portugal; 2. The Chronicle of the Cid; 3. The Curse of Kehama; 4. Espriella's Letters. Look you, all these *I am* writing. . . . . By way of interlude comes in this preface. Don't swear, and bid me do one thing at a time. I tell you I can't afford to do one thing at a time—no, nor two neither; and it is only by doing many things that I contrive to do so much: for I cannot work long together at anything without hurting myself, and so I do everything by heats; then,

by the time I am tired of one, my inclination for another
is come round." A strong deliberate energy accordingly
is at the back of all Southey's work ; but not that blind
creative rapture which will have its own way, and leaves
its subject weak but appeased. " In the daytime I
laboured," says Landor, "and at night unburdened my
soul, shedding many tears. My *Tiberius* has so shaken
me at last that the least thing affects me violently."
Southey shrank back from such agitations. A great
Elizabethan poet is described by one of his contemporaries as standing

> Up to the chin in the Pierian flood.

Southey did not wade so far ; he stepped down calmly
until the smooth waters touched his waist; dipped seven
times, and returned to the bank ; it was a beautiful and
an elevating rite ; but the waves sing with lyric lips only
in the midmost stream, and he who sings with them, and
as swift as they, need not wonder if he sink after a time,
faint, breathless, delighted.

Authorship, it must be remembered, was Southey's trade,
the business of his life, and this at least he knew how to
conduct well. To be a prophet and call down flame from
heaven, and disappear in a whirlwind and a chariot of fire
is sublime ; but prophets can go in the strength of a single
meal for more days and nights than one would choose to
name in this incredulous age, and, if they eat, there are
ravens to bring them food. No ravens brought loaves to
Greta Hall, and Southey had an unprophet-like craving
for the creature comforts of beef and bread, for wine if it
might be had, and at supper for one meditative tumbler of
punch or black currant rum. Besides, what ravens were
ever pledged to feed a prophet's sisters-in-law, or his

nephews and nieces? Let it be praise enough for much
of Southey's performance, that he did good work in work-
manlike fashion. To shift knowledge into more con-
venient positions is to render no unimportant service to
mankind. In the gathering of facts, Southey was both
swift and patient in an extraordinary degree; he went
often alone, and he went far; in the art of exposition he
was unsurpassed; and his fine moral feeling and profound
sympathy with elementary justice created, as De Quincey
has observed, a soul under what else might well be de-
nominated, Miltonically, "the ribs of death." From the
mending of his pens to the second reading aloud of his
proof-sheets, attending as he read to the fall of each
word upon the ear, Southey had a diligent care for
everything that served to make his work right. He wrote
at a moderate pace; re-wrote; wrote a third time if it
seemed desirable; corrected with minute supervision. He
accomplished so much, not because he produced with unexampled rapidity, but because he worked regularly, and
never fell into a mood of apathy or ennui. No periods
of tempestuous vacancy lay between his periods of patient
labour. One work always overlapped another—thus, that
first idle day, the begetter of so many idle descendants,
never came. But let us hear the craftsman giving a lesson
in the knack of authorship to his brother, Dr. Henry
Southey, who has a notion of writing something on the
Crusades :—

Now then, supposing that you will seriously set about the
Crusades, I will give you such directions in the art of historical
book-keeping as may save time and facilitate labour.

Make your writing books in foolscap quarto, and write on
only one side of a leaf; draw a line down the margin, marking
off space enough for your references, which should be given at

the end of every paragraph;—noting page, book, or chapter of
the author referred to. This minuteness is now demanded, and
you will yourself find it useful; for in transcribing or in correcting proofs, it is often requisite to turn to the original authorities.
Take the best author, that is to say the one that has written
most at length of all the *original* authors, upon the particular
point of time on which you are employed, and draw up your
account from him; then, on the opposite page, correct and
amplify this from every other who has written on the same
subject. This page should be divided into two columns, one of
about two-thirds of its breadth, the other the remaining one.
You are thus enabled to *add* to your *additions*.

One of these books you should have for your geography; that
is to say, for collecting descriptions of all the principal scenes of
action (which must be done from books of travels), their situation,
their strength, their previous history, and in the notes, their
present state. [Another book—he adds in a subsequent letter—
you must keep for the bibliography of your subject.]

These descriptions you can insert in their proper places when
you transcribe. Thus, also, you should collect accounts of the
different tribes and dynasties which you have occasion to mention.
In this manner the information which is only to be got at
piecemeal, and oftentimes incidentally, when you are looking
for something else, is brought together with least trouble, and
almost imperceptibly.

All relative matter, not absolutely essential to the subject,
should go in the form of supplementary notes, and these you
may make as amusing as you please, the more so, and the more
curious, the better. Much trouble is saved by writing them on
separate bits of paper, each the half of a quarter of a foolscap
sheet,—numbering them, and making an index of them; in this
manner they are ready for use when they are wanted.

It was some time before I fell unto this system of book-
keeping, and I believe no better can be desired. A Welsh triad
might comprehend all the rules of style. Say what you have
to say as *perspicuously* as possible, as *briefly* as possible, and
as *rememberably* as possible, and take no other thought about
it. Omit none of those little circumstances which give life to

narration, and bring old manners, old feelings, and old times before your eyes.

Winter was Southey's harvest season. Then for weeks no visitor knocked at Greta Hall, except perhaps Mr. Wordsworth, who had plodded all the way from Rydal on his indefatigable legs. But in summer interruptions were frequent, and Southey, who had time for every-thing, had time to spare not only for friends but for strangers. The swarm of lakers was indeed not what it is now-a-days, but to a studious man it was perhaps not less formidable. By Gray's time the secret of the lakes had been found out; and if the visitors were fewer, they were less swift upon the wing, and their rank or fame often entitled them to particular attention. Coroneted coaches rolled into Keswick, luggage-laden; the American arrived sometimes to make sure that Derwentwater would not be missed out of Lake Michigan, sometimes to see King George's laureate; and cultured Americans were par-ticularly welcome to Southey. Long-vacation reading-parties from Oxford and Cambridge—known among the good Cumberland folk as the " cathedrals"—made Keswick a resort. Well for them if provided with an introduc-tion, they were invited to dine at Greta Hall, were permitted to gaze on the choice old Spaniards and to converse with the laureate's stately Edith and her learned cousin. Woe to them if after the entanglements of a Greek chorus or descriptions of the temperate man and the mag-nanimous man, they sought to restore their tone by a cat-worrying expedition among the cottages of Keswick. Southey's cheek glowed, his eye darkened and flashed if he chanced to witness cruelty; some of the Cambridge " cathedrals" who received a letter concerning cats in July, 1834, may still bear the mark of its leaded thong in their

moral fibre, and be the better for possessing Southey's
sign-manual.

A young step-child of Oxford visited Keswick in the
winter of 1811-12, and sought the acquaintance of the
author of *Thalaba*. Had Southey been as intolerant or
as unsympathetic as some have represented him, he could
not have endured the society of one so alien in opinion
and so outspoken as Shelley. But courtesy, if it were
nothing more, was at least part of Southey's self-respect ;
his intolerance towards persons was in truth towards a
certain ideal, a certain group of opinions; when hand
touched hand and eye met eye all intolerance vanished,
and he was open to every gracious attraction of character
and manner. There was much in Shelley that could not
fail to interest Southey ; both loved poetry, and both felt
the proud, secluded grandeur of Landor's verse ; both loved
men, and thought the world wants mending, though their
plans of reform might differ. That Shelley was a rebel
expelled from Oxford did not shock Southey, who himself had been expelled from Westminster and rejected at
Christ Church. Shelley's opinions were crude and violent,
but their spirit was generous, and such opinions held by
a youth in his teens generally mean no more than that
his brain is working and his heart ardent. Shelley's
rash marriage reminded Southey of another marriage,
celebrated at Bristol some fifteen years ago, which proved
that rashness is not always folly. The young man's admiration of *Thalaba* spoke well for him ; and certainly
during the earlier weeks of their intercourse there was on
Shelley's part a becoming deference to one so much his
superior in years and in learning, deference to one who had
achieved much while Shelley still only dreamed of achievement. Southey thought he saw in the revolutionary en-

thusiast an image of his former self. " Here," he says, " is a
man at Keswick who acts upon me as my own ghost would
do.   He is just what I was in 1794.   His name is Shelley,
son to the member for Shoreham. . . . . At present he has
got to the Pantheistic stage of philosophy, and in the course
of a week I expect he will be a Berkeleyan, for I have put
him upon a course of Berkeley.   It has surprised him a
good deal to meet, for the first time in his life, with a man
who perfectly understands him and does him full justice.
I tell him that all the difference between us is that he is
nineteen and I am thirty-seven ; and I daresay it will not
be very long before I shall succeed in convincing him that
he may be a true philosopher and do a great deal of good
with 6000*l.* a year ; the thought of which troubles him a
great deal more at present than ever the want of sixpence
(for I have known such a want) did me."   There were
other differences between Robert Southey and the incon-
stant star that passed by Greta Hall than that of years.
Southey had quickly learned to put a bound to his desires,
and within that bound to work out for himself a possession of measureless worth.   It seemed to him part of a
man's virtue to adhere loyally to the bond signed for each
of us when we enter life.   Is our knowledge limited,—
then let us strive within those limits.   Can we never lay
hands on the absolute good—then let us cherish the
good things that are ours.   Do we hold our dearest possessions on a limited tenure—that is hard, but is it not
in the bond ?   How faint a loyalty is his who merely
yields obedience perforce ; let us rather cast in our will,
unadulterate and whole, with that of our divine Leader ;
sursum corda—there is a heaven above.   But Shelley—
the nympholept of some radiant ante-natal sphere—fled
through his brief years ever in pursuit of his lost lady of

light ; and for him loyalty to the bond of life seemed to
mean a readiness to forget all things, however cherished,
so soon as they had fulfilled their service of speeding
him on towards the unattainable.   It could not but be
that men living under rules so diverse should before long
find themselves far asunder.   But they parted in 1812
in no spirit of ill-will.   Southey was already a state-
pensioner and a champion of the party of order in the
Quarterly Review; this did not prevent the young apostle
of liberty and fraternity from entering his doors, and
enjoying Mrs. Southey's tea-cakes.   Irish affairs were
earnestly discussed, but Southey, who had written gene-
rously of Emmett both in his verse and in the *Quarterly*,
could not be hostile to one whose illusions were only over-
sanguine ; and while the veritable Southey was before
Shelley's eyes, he could not discern the dull hireling, the
venomous apostate, the cold-blooded assassin of freedom
conjured up by Byron and others to bear Southey's name.

Three years later Shelley presented his *Alastor* to
the laureate, and Southey duly acknowledged the gift.
The elder poet was never slow to recognize genius in
young men, but conduct was to him of higher importance
than genius ; he deplored some acts in Shelley's life which
seemed to result directly from opinions professed at Keswick in 1811—opinions then interpreted as no more than
the disdain of checks felt by every spirited boy.   Southey
heard no more from him until a letter came from Pisa
inquiring whether Shelley's former entertainer at Keswick
were his recent critic of the *Quarterly Review*, with added
comments, courteous but severe, on Southey's opinions.   The
reply was that Southey had not written the paper, and had
never in any of his writings alluded to Shelley in any way.
A second letter followed on each side, the elder man plead-

ing, exhorting, warning ; the younger justifying himself,
and returning to the attack. " There the correspondence
ended. On Shelley's part it was conducted with the courtesy which was natural to him ; on mine, in the spirit of
one who was earnestly admonishing a fellow-creature."

Much of Southey's time—his most valued possession—
was given to his correspondents. Napoleon's plan of answering letters, according to Bourrienne, was to let them lie
unopened for six weeks, by which time nine out of ten had
answered themselves, or had been answered by history.
Coleridge's plan—says De Quincey—was shorter ; he
opened none, and answered none. To answer all forthwith was the habit of Southey. Thinking doubtless of
their differences in such minor moralities of life, Coleridge
writes of his brother-in-law :—" Always employed, his
friends find him always at leisure. No less punctual in
trifles, than steadfast in the performance of highest duties,
he inflicts none of those small pains which irregular men
scatter about them, and which in the aggregate so often
become formidable obstacles both to happiness and utility ;
while on the contrary he bestows all the pleasures and
inspires all that ease of mind on those around or connected
with him, which perfect consistency and (if such a word
might be framed) absolute *reliability*, equally in small as
in great concerns, cannot but inspire and bestow ; when
this too is softened without being weakened by kindness
and gentleness." Odd indeed were some of the communi-
cations for which the poet laureate, the Tory reformer, and
the loyal son of the Church was the mark. Now a clergyman writes to furnish him with Scriptural illustrations of
Thalaba ; now another clergyman favours him with an
ingenious parallel between Kehama and Nebuchadnezzar ;
now some anonymous person seriously urges on Southey

his duty of making a new version of the Psalms, and laying it before the King to be approved and appointed to be sung in churches ; now a lunatic poet desires his brother to procure for his title-page the names of Messrs. Longman and Rees; now a poor woman, wife to a blind Homer, would have him led carefully to the summit of Parnassus ; now a poor French devil volunteers to translate *Roderick* if the author will have the goodness to send him a copy—even a defective copy—which he pledges himself religiously to return ; now a Yankee who keeps an exhibition at Philadelphia, modestly asks for Southey's painted portrait " which is very worthy a place in my collection ; " now a herdsman in the vale of Clwyd requests permission to send specimens of prose and verse —his highest ambition is the acquaintance of learned men ; now the Rev. Peter Hall begs to inform Southey that he has done more harm to the cause of religion than any writer of the age ; now a lover requests him to make an acrostic on the name of a young lady—the lover's rival has beaten him in writing verses ; enclosed is the honorarium.   Southey's amiability at this point gave way ; he did not write the acrostic, and the money he spent on blankets for poor women in Keswick. A society for the suppression of albums was proposed by Southey ; yet sometimes he was captured in the gracious mood. Samuel Simpson of Liverpool begs for a few lines in his handwriting " to fill a vacancy in his collection of autographs, without which his series must remain for ever most incomplete."   The laureate replies :—

> Inasmuch as you Sam, a descendant of Sim,
> For collecting handwritings have taken a whim,
> And to me, Robert Southey, petition have made,
> In a civil and nicely-penned letter—post-paid,—

> That I to your album so gracious would be
> As to fill up a page there appointed for me,
> Five couplets I send you, by aid of the Nine—
> They will cost you in postage a penny a line,
> At Keswick, October the sixth, they were done,
> One thousand eight hundred and twenty and one.

Some of Southey's distractions were of his own inviting. Soon after his arrival at Keswick, a tiny volume of poems entitled *Clifton Grove* attracted his attention ; its author was an undergraduate of Cambridge. The Monthly Review having made the discovery that it rhymed in one place *boy* and *sky* dismissed the book contemptuously. Southey could not bear to think that the hopes of a lad of promise should be blasted, and he wrote to Henry Kirke White, encouraging him and offering him help towards a future volume. The cruel dulness of the reviewer sat heavily on the poor boy's spirits, and these unexpected words of cheer came with most grateful effect. It soon appeared, however, that Southey's services must be slight, for his new acquaintance was taken out of his hands by Mr. Simeon, the nursing-father of Evangelicalism. At no time had Southey any leanings toward the Clapham Sect; and so while he tried to be of use to Kirke White indirectly, their correspondence ceased. When the lad, in every way lacking pith and substance, and ripening prematurely in a heated atmosphere, drooped and died, Southey was not willing that he should be altogether forgotten; he wrote offering to look over whatever papers there might be, and to give an opinion on them "Down came a box-full," he tells Duppa, "the sight of which literally made my heart ache, and my eyes overflow, for never did I behold such proofs of human industry. To make short, I took the matter up with interest, collected his letters, and have, at the expense of more time than

such a poor fellow as myself can very well afford, done
what his family are very grateful for, and what I think
the world will thank me for too. Of course I have done
it gratuitously. . . . That I should become and that
voluntarily too, an editor of Methodistical and Calvinistic
letters, is a thing which when I think of excites the same
sort of smile that the thought of my pension does." A brief
statement that his own views on religion differed widely
from those of Kirke White sufficed to save Southey's in-
tegrity. The genius of the dead poet he over-rated; it was
an error which the world has since found time to correct.

This was but one of a series of many instances in which
Southey, stemming the pressure of his own engagements,
asserted the right to be generous of his time and strength
and substance to those who had need of such help as a
sound heart and a strong arm can give. William Roberts,
a Bristol bank-clerk, dying of consumption at nineteen, left
his only possession, some manuscript poems, in trust to be
published for the benefit of a sister whom he passionately
loved. Southey was consulted, and at once bestirred himself on behalf of the projected volume. Herbert Knowles,
an orphan lad at school in Yorkshire, had hoped to go as
a sizar to St. John's; his relations were unable to send
him; could he help himself by publishing a poem? might
he dedicate it to the laureate? The poem came to Southey,
who found it "brimful of power and of promise;" he
represented to Herbert the folly of publishing, promised
ten pounds himself and procured from Rogers and Earl
Spencer twenty more. Herbert Knowles, in a wise and
manly letter, begged that great things might not be expected of him; he would not be idle, his University career
should be at least respectable: "Suffice it, then, to say *I
thank you from my heart;* let time and my future conduct

tell the rest." Death came to arbitrate between his hopes and fears. James Dusautoy, another schoolboy, one of ten children of a retired officer, sent specimens of his verse, asking Southey's opinion on certain poetical plans; his friends thought the law the best profession for him; how could he make literature help him forward in his profession? Southey again advised against publication, but by a well-timed effort enabled him to enter Emanuel College. Dusautoy, after a brilliant promise, took fever, died, and was buried, in acknowledgment of his character and talents, in the college cloisters. When at Harrogate in the summer of 1827, Southey received a letter, written with much modesty and good feeling, from John Jones, an old serving-man; he enclosed a poem on "The Redbreast," and would take the liberty, if permitted, to offer other manuscripts for inspection. Touches of true observation and natural feeling in the verses on the little bird with "look oblique and prying head and gentle affability" pleased Southey, and he told his humble applicant to send his manuscript book, warning him, however, not to expect that such poems would please the public—"the time for them was gone by, and whether the public had grown wiser in these matters or not, it had certainly become less tolerant and less charitable." By procuring subscribers and himself contributing an Introductory Essay on the lives and works of our Uneducated Poets, Southey secured a siender fortune for the worthy old man, who laid the table none the less punctually because he loved Shakspere and the Psalter, or carried in his head some simple rhymes of his own. It pleased Southey to show how much intellectual pleasure and moral improvement connected with such pleasure are within reach of the humblest; thus a lesson was afforded to those who would have the March of Intellect beaten

only to the tune of *Ça ira.* "Before I conclude"—so
the Introduction draws to an end—"I must, in my
own behalf, give notice to all whom it may concern
that I, Robert Southey, Poet Laureate, being somewhat advanced in years, and having business enough of
my own fully to occupy as much time as can be devoted
to it, consistently with a due regard to health, do hereby
decline perusing or inspecting any manuscript from any
person whatsoever, and desire that no application on that
score may be made to me from this time forth ; this resolution, which for most just cause is taken and here notified,
being, like the laws of the Medes and the Persians, not to
be changed."

It was some time after this public announcement that
a hand, which may have trembled while yet it was very
brave and resolute, dropped into the little post-office at
Haworth in Yorkshire a packet for Robert Southey.
His bold truthfulness, his masculine self-control, his strong
heart, his domestic temper sweet and venerable, his purity
of manners, a certain sweet austerity, attracted to him
women of fine sensibility and genius who would fain escape
from their own falterings and temerities under the authority
of a faithful director. Already Maria del Occidente, "the
most impassioned and most imaginative of all poetesses,"
had poured into his ear the tale of her slighted love.
Newly come from Paris, and full of enthusiasm for the
Poles, she hastened to Keswick to see in person her sym-
pathetic adviser ; she proved, says Southey, a most in-
teresting person of the mildest and gentlest manners. With
him she left, on returning to America, her *Zophiel* in
manuscript, the publication of which he superintended.
"*Zophiel*, Southey says, is by some Yankee woman"—
Charles Lamb breaks forth—"as if there ever had been

K

a woman capable of anything so great!" Now, in 1837,
a woman of finer spirit and capable of higher things than
Zophiel, addressed a letter to Robert Southey, asking his
judgment of her powers as disclosed in the poems which
she forwarded. For some weeks Charlotte Brontë waited,
until almost all hope of a reply was lost. At length the
verdict came. Charlotte Brontë's verse was assuredly written with her left hand; her passionate impulses, crossed
and checked by fiery fiats of the will, would not mould
themselves into little stanzas; the little stanzas must be
correct, therefore they must reject such irregular heavings
and swift repressions of the heart. Southey's delay in
replying had been caused by absence from home. A
little personal knowledge of a poet in the decline of life
might have tempered her enthusiasm; yet he is neither
a disappointed nor a discontented man; she will never
hear from him any chilling sermons on the text, All is
vanity; the faculty of verse she possesses in no inconsiderable degree; but this since the beginning of the
century has grown to be no rare possession; let her beware
of making literature her profession, check day-dreams,
and find her chief happiness in her womanly duties;
then she may write poetry for its own sake, not in a spirit
of emulation, not through a passion for celebrity; the less
celebrity is aimed at the more it is likely to be deserved.
" Mr. Southey's letter," said Charlotte Brontë, many years
later, " was kind and admirable, a little stringent, but it
did me good." She wrote again, striving to repress a
palpitating joy and pride in the submission to her director's counsel, and the sacrifice of her cherished hopes;
telling him more of her daily life, of her obedience to the
day's duty, her efforts to be sensible and sober: " I had
not ventured," she says, " to hope for such a reply; so

considerate in its tone, so noble in its spirit." Once more
Southey wrote hoping that she would let him see her at
the Lakes : " You would then think of me afterwards
with the more good-will, because you would perceive that
there is neither severity nor moroseness in the state of
mind to which years and observation have brought me.
. . . . And now, madam, God bless you. Farewell, and
believe me to be your sincere friend, Robert Southey."
It was during a visit to the Lakes that Charlotte Brontë
told her biographer of these letters. But Southey lay at
rest in Crosthwaite churchyard.

"My days among the dead are past,"—Southey wrote,
but it is evident that the living, and not those of his own
household alone, claimed no inconsiderable portion of his
time. Indeed it would not be untrue to assert that few
men have been more genuinely and consistently social,
that few men ever yielded themselves more constantly to
the pleasures of companionship. But the society he loved
best was that of old and chosen friends, or if new friends,
one at a time and only one. Next to romping with my
children, he said, I enjoy a tête-à-tête conversation with an
old friend or a *new*. " With one I can talk of familiar
subjects which we have discussed in former years, and with
the other, if he have any brains, I open what to me is a new
mine of thought." Miscellaneous company to a certain extent disordered and intoxicated him. He felt no temptation
to say a great deal, but he would often say things strongly
and emphatically, which were better left unsaid. " In my
hearty hatred of assentation I commit faults of the opposite
kind. Now I am sure to find this out myself and to get
out of humour with myself ; what prudence I have is not
ready on demand ; and so it is that the society of any
except my friends though it may be sweet in the mouth is

bitter in the belly." When Coleridge, in their arguments,
allowed him a word, Southey made up in weight for what
was wanting in measure; he saw one fact quickly, and
darted at it like a greyhound. De Quincey has described
his conversation as less flowing and expansive than that of
Wordsworth—more apt to clothe itself in a keen, sparkling,
aphoristic form; consequently sooner coming to an abrupt
close; "the style of his mind naturally prompts him to
adopt a trenchant, pungent, aculeated form of terse, glittering, stenographic sentences—sayings which have the
air of laying down the law without any *locus penitentiæ*
or privilege of appeal, but are not meant to do so." The
same manner tempered and chastened by years can be
recognized in the picture of Southey drawn by his friend
Sir Henry Taylor :—

The characteristics of his manner, as of his appearance, were
lightness and strength, an easy and happy composure as the
accustomed mood, and much mobility at the same time, so that
he could be readily excited into any degree of animation in discourse, speaking, if the subject moved him much, with extraordinary fire and force, though always in light, laconic sentences.
When so moved, the fingers of his right hand often rested
against his mouth and quivered through nervous susceptibility.
But excitable as he was in conversation, he was never angry or
irritable; nor can there be any greater mistake concerning him,
than that into which some persons have fallen when they have
inferred, from the fiery vehemence with which he could give
utterance to moral anger in verse or prose, that he was personally
ill-tempered or irascible. He was in truth a man whom it was
hardly possible to quarrel with or offend personally and face to
face. . . . . He was averse from argumentation and would
commonly quit a subject when it was passing into that shape,
with a quiet and good-humoured indication of the view in which
he rested. He talked most, and with most interest about books,
and about public affairs; less, indeed hardly at all, about the

characters and qualities of men in private life. In the society of strangers or of acquaintances, he seemed to take more interest in the subjects spoken of than in the persons present, his manner being that of natural courtesy and general benevolence without distinction of individuals. Had there been some tincture of social vanity in him, perhaps he would have been brought into closer relations with those whom he met in society ; but though invariably kind and careful of their feelings, he was indifferent to the manner in which they regarded him, or (as the phrase is) to his *effect* in society; and they might perhaps be conscious that the kindness they received was what flowed naturally and inevitably to all, that they had nothing to give in return which was of value to him, and that no individual relations were established.

How deep and rich Southey's social nature was his published correspondence, some four or five thousand printed pages, tells sufficiently. These letters, addressed for the most part to good old friends, are indeed genial, liberal of sympathy, and expecting sympathy in return, pleasantly egoistic, grave, playful, wise, pathetic with a kind of stringent pathos showing through checks imposed by the wiser and stronger will. Southey did not squander abroad the treasures of his affection. To lavish upon casual acquaintance the outward and visible signs of friendship seemed to him a profaning of the mystery of manly love. " Your feelings," he writes to Coleridge, "go naked, I cover mine with a bear-skin ; I will not say that you harden yours by your mode, but I am sure that mine are the warmer for their clothing." With strangers a certain neutral courtesy served to protect his inner self like the low leaves of his own holly tree :

> Below, a circling fence, its leaves are seen
> Wrinkled and keen ;
> No grazing cattle through their prickly round
> Can reach to wound ;

but to those of whose goodness and love he was well
assured, there were no protecting spines :

> Gentle at home amid my friends I'd be
> Like the high leaves upon the Holly Tree.

"Old friends and old books," he says, "are the best
things that this world affords (I like old wine also), and in
these I am richer than most men (the wine excepted)."
In the group of Southey's friends, what first strikes one is
not that they are men of genius—although the group in-
cludes Wordsworth and Scott, and Henry Taylor—but
that they are good men. No one believed more thoroughly
than Southey that goodness is a better thing than genius ;
yet he required in his associates some high excellence,
extraordinary kindness of disposition or strength of moral
character, if not extraordinary intellect. To knit his friends
in a circle was his ardent desire; in the strength of his
affections time and distance made no change. An old
College friend, Lightfoot, to visit Southey made the
longest journey of his life ; it was eight and twenty years
since they had met. When their hands touched, Lightfoot
trembled like an aspen-leaf. "I believe," says Southey,
"no men ever met more cordially after so long a separation,
or enjoyed each other's society more. I shall never forget
the manner in which he first met me, nor the tone in
which he said 'that, having now seen me, he should
return home and die in peace.'" But of all friends he was
most at ease with his dear Dapple, Grosvenor Bedford,
who suited for every mood of mirth and sorrow. When
Mrs. Southey had fallen into her sad decay, and the
once joyous house was melancholy and silent, Southey
turned for comfort to Bedford. Still some of their
Rabelaisian humour remained, and all their warmth of

brotherly affection. " My father," says Cuthbert Southey,
" was never tired of talking into Mr. Bedford's trumpet." And in more joyous days, what noise and nonsense did they not make ! " Oh ! Grosvenor," exclaims
Southey, " is it not a pity that two men who love
nonsense so cordially and naturally and *bonâfidically* as
you and I, should be three hundred miles asunder ? For
my part I insist upon it that there is no sense so good as
your honest genuine nonsense."

A goodly company of friends becomes familiar to us as
we read Southey's correspondence; Wynn, wherever he
was, " always doing something else," yet able in the
midst of politics and business to find time to serve an old
schoolfellow ; Rickman, full of practical suggestions, and
accurate knowledge and robust benevolence ; John May,
unfailing in kindness and fidelity ; Lamb for play and
pathos, and subtle criticism glancing amid the puns ; William Taylor for culture and literary theory, and paradox
and polysyllables ; Landor for generous admiration, and
kindred enthusiasms and kindred prejudices ; Elmsley and
Lightfoot and Danvers for love and happy memories ;
Senhora Barker, the Bhow Begum, for frank familiarities,
and warm, womanly services ; Caroline Bowles for rarer
sympathy and sacreder hopes and fears ; Henry Taylor for
spiritual sonship as of a son who is also an equal ; and
Grosvenor Bedford, for everything great and small, glad
and sad, wise and foolish.

No literary rivalries or jealousies ever interrupted for a
moment any friendship of Southey. Political and religious differences, which in strangers were causes of grave
offence, seemed to melt away when the heretic or erring
statist was a friend. But if success, fashion, flattery tested
a man, and proved him wanting, as seemed to be the case

with Humphrey Davy, his affection grew cold; and an habitual dereliction of social duty, such as that of Coleridge, could not but transform Southey's feeling of love to one of condemning sorrow. To his great contemporaries, Scott, Landor, Wordsworth, his admiration was freely given. "Scott," he writes, "is very ill. He suffers dreadfully; but bears his sufferings with admirable equanimity. . . . God grant that he may recover! He is a noble and generous-hearted creature, whose like we shall not look upon again." Of Wordsworth: "A greater poet than Wordsworth there never has been, nor ever will be:" "Two or three genera-tions must pass before the public affect to admire such poets as Milton and Wordsworth. Of such men the world scarcely produces one in a millennium." With indignation crossed by a gleam of humour, he learnt that Ebenezer Elliott, his pupil in the art of verse, had stepped forward as the lyrist of radicalism; but the feeling could not be altogether anger with which he remembered that earnest face, once seen by him at a Sheffield inn, its pale grey eyes full of fire and meaning, its expression suiting well with Elliott's frankness of manner, and simplicity of character. William Taylor was one of the liberals of liberal Norwich, and dangled abroad whatever happened to be the newest paradox in religion. But neither his radicalism, nor his Pyrrhonism, nor his paradoxes could estrange Southey. The last time the oddly-assorted pair met was in Taylor's house; the student of German criticism had found some theological novelty, and wished to draw his guest into argument; Southey parried the thrusts good-humouredly, and at last put an end to them with the words, "Taylor, come and see me at Keswick. We will ascend Skiddaw. where I shall have you nearer heaven, and we will then discuss such questions as these."

In the year 1823 one of his oldest friends made a public attack on Southey, and that friend the gentlest and
sweetest-natured of them all.   In a *Quarterly* article
Southey had spoken of the Essays of Elia as a book
which wanted only a sounder religious feeling to be as
delightful as it was original.   He had intended to alter
the expression in the proof-sheet, but no proof-sheet
was ever sent.   Lamb, already pained by references to his
writings in the *Quarterly*, some of which he erroneously
ascribed to Southey, was deeply wounded.   " He might
have spared an old friend such a construction of a
few careless flights, that meant no harm to religion."
A long expostulation addressed by Elia to Robert Southey,
Esq., appeared in the London Magazine for October,
only a portion of which is retained in the Elia Essays
under the title of "The Tombs of the Abbey;" for
though Lamb had playfully resented Coleridge's salutation, " my gentle-hearted Charles," his heart was indeed
gentle, and could not endure the pain of its own wrath;
among the memorials of the dead in Westminster he finds
his right mind, his truer self once more; he forgets the
grave aspect with which Southey looked awful on his
poor friend, and spends his indignation harmless as summer lightning over the heads of a Dean and Chapter.
Southey, seeing the announcement of a letter addressed to
him by Lamb, had expected a sheaf of friendly pleasantries;
with surprise he learnt what pain his words had caused.
He hastened to explain; had Lamb intimated his feelings
in private, he would have tried, by a passage in the ensu-
ing *Quarterly*, to efface the impression unhappily created;
he ended with a declaration of unchanged affection, and
a proposal to call on Lamb.   " On my part," Southey
said, " there was not even a momentary feeling of

anger;" he at once understood the love, the error, the
soreness, and the repentance awaiting a being so composed of goodness as Elia. "Dear Southey"—runs
the° answer of Lamb—"the kindness of your note has
melted away the mist that was upon me. I have been
fighting against a shadow. . . . . I wish both magazine
and review were at the bottom of the sea. I shall be
ashamed to see you, and my sister (though innocent) will
be still more so, for this folly was done without her knowledge, and has made her uneasy ever since. My guardian
angel was absent at the time. I will make up courage to
see you, however, any day next week. We shall hope
that you will bring Edith with you. That will be a second
mortification; she will hate to see us; but come and heap
embers; we deserve it, I for what I have done, and she
for being my sister. Do come early in the day by sunlight that you may see my Milton. . . . . Your penitent
C. Lamb."

At Bristol in 1808 Southey met for the first time the
man of all others whom he most desired to see, the only
man living, he says, " of whose praise I was ambitious, or
whose censure would have humbled me." This was Walter
Savage Landor. *Madoc*, on which Southey had built his
hope of renown as a poet, had been published, and had
been coldly received ;˙ *Kehama*, which had been begun,
consequently now stood still. Their author could indeed,
as he told Sir George Beaumont, be contented with posthumous fame, but it was impossible to be contented with
posthumous bread and cheese. " St. Cecilia herself could
not have played the organ if there had been nobody to
blow the bellows for her." At this moment, when he
turned sadly and bravely from poetry to more profitable
work he first looked on Landor. "I never saw any

one more unlike myself," he writes, "in every prominent
part of human character, nor any one who so cordially
and instinctively agreed with me on so many of the
most important subjects. I have often said before we
met, that I would walk forty miles to see him, and
having seen him, I would gladly walk fourscore to see
him again. He talked of *Thalaba*, and I told him of
the series of mythological poems which I had planned,
. . . . and also told him for what reason they had been
laid aside ;—in plain English, that I could not afford to
write them. Landor's reply was, ' Go on with them, and I
will pay for printing them, as many as you will write, and
as many copies as you please.' "   The princely offer stung
Southey, as he says, to the very core ; not that he thought
of accepting that offer, but the generous words were themselves a deed and claimed a return.   He rose earlier each
morning to carry on his *Kehama*, without abstracting time
from better-paid task-work ; it advanced, and duly as each
section of this poem, and subsequently of his *Roderick*, came
to be written, it was transcribed for the friend whose sympathy and admiration were a golden reward. To be praised
by one's peers is indeed happiness. Landor, liberal of applause, was keen in suggestion and exact in censure. Both
friends were men of ardent feelings, though one had
tamed himself, while the other never could be tamed ;
both often gave their feelings a vehement utterance.
On many matters they thought in the main alike—on
the grand style in human conduct, on the principles of
the poetic art, on Spanish affairs, on Catholicism. The
secret of Landor's high-poised dignity in verse had been
discovered by Southey; he, like Landor, aimed at a
classical purity of diction ; he, like Landor, loved, as a
shaper of imaginative forms, to embody in an act, or an

incident, the virtue of some eminent moment of human
passion, and to give it fixity by sculptured phrase; only
the repression of a fiery spirit is more apparent in Landor's monumental lines than in Southey's. With certain
organic resemblances, and much community of sentiment,
there were large differences between the two, so that when
they were drawn together in sympathy, each felt as if he
had annexed a new province. Landor rejoiced that the
first persons who shared his turret at Llanthony were
Southey and his wife; again, in 1817, the two friends
were together for three days at Como, after Southey had
endured his prime affliction—the death of his son :—

> Grief had swept over him; days darkened round;
> Bellagio, Valintelvi smiled in vain,
> And Monte Rosa from Helvetia far
> Advanced to meet us, wild in majesty
> Above the glittering crests of giant sons
> Station'd around . . . in vain too! all in vain.

Two years later the warm-hearted friend writes from
Pistoia, rejoicing in Southey's joy: " Thank God ! Tears
came into my eyes on seeing that you were blessed with
a son." To watch the happiness of children was Landor's
highest delight, to share in such happiness was Southey's,
and Arnold and Cuthbert formed a new bond between their
fathers. In 1836, when Southey, in his sixty-third year,
guided his son through the scenes of his boyhood, several
delightful days were spent at Clifton with Landor. I
never knew a man of brighter genius or of kinder heart,
said Southey ; and of Landor in earlier years : " He does
more than any of the gods of all my mythologies, for his
very words are thunder and lightning—such is the power
and splendour with which they burst out." Landor
responded with a majestic enthusiasm about his friend,

who seemed to him no less noble a man than admirable a
writer :—

> No firmer breast than thine hath Heaven
>   To poet, sage, or hero given :
> No heart more tender, none more just,
>   To that He largely placed in trust :
> Therefore shalt thou, whatever date
> Of years be thine, with soul elate
> Rise up before the Eternal throne,
> And hear, in God's own voice, " Well done."

That " Well done" greeted Southey many years before
Landor's imperial head was laid low. In the last letter
from his friend received by Southey—already the darkness
was fast closing in—he writes, " If any man living is
ardent for your welfare, I am; whose few and almost
worthless merits your generous heart has always over-
valued, and whose infinite and great faults it has been too
ready to overlook. I will write to you often, now I learn
that I may do it inoffensively ; well remembering that
among the names you have exalted is Walter Landor."
Alas! to reply was now beyond the power of Southey ;
still he held *Gebir* in his hands oftener than any other
volume of poetry, and while thought and feeling lived, fed
upon its beauty. " It is very seldom now," Caroline
Southey wrote at a later date, " that he ever names any
person : but this morning, before he left his bed, I heard
him repeating softly to himself *Landor, ay, Landor.*"

" If it be not now, yet it will come : the readiness is all "
—this was ever present to Southey during the happy days
of labour and rest in Greta Hall. While he was disposing
his books so as to make the comeliest show, and delighting
in their goodly ranks, while he looked into the radiant faces
of his children, and loved their innocent brightness, he yet

knew that the day of detachment was approaching. There
was nothing in such a thought which stirred Southey to a
rebellious mood; had he not set his seal to the bond of
life? How his heart rested in his home, only his own
words can tell; even a journey to London seemed too
long:—" Oh, dear; oh, dear! there is such a comfort in
one's old coat and old shoes, one's own chair and own
fireside, one's own writing-desk and own library,—with a
little girl climbing up to my neck, and saying, ' Don't go
to London, papa—you must stay with Edith ' ; and a little
boy, whom I have taught to speak the language of cats,
dogs, cuckoos, and jackasses, &c., before he can articulate
a word of his own ;—there is such a comfort in all these
things, that *transportation* to London for four or five
weeks seems a heavier punishment than any sins of mine
deserve." Nor did his spirit of boyish merriment abate
until overwhelming sorrow weighed him down : " I am
quite as noisy as I ever was," he writes to Lightfoot, "and
should take as much delight as ever in showering stones
through the hole of the staircase against your room door,
and hearing with what hearty good earnest ' you fool ' was
vociferated in indignation against me in return. O, dear
Lightfoot, what a blessing it is to have a boy's heart ! it
is as great a blessing in carrying one through this world,
as to have a child's spirit will be in fitting us for the
next." But Southey's light-heartedness was rounded by
a circle of earnest acquiescence in the law of mortal life ;
a clear-obscure of faith as pure and calm and grave as the
heavens of a midsummer night. At thirty he writes :—
" No man was ever more contented with his lot than I am,
for few have ever had more enjoyments, and none had
ever better or worthier hopes. Life, therefore, is sufficiently dear to me, and long life desirable, that I may

accomplish all which I design.   But yet, I could be well
content that the next century were over, and my part
fairly at an end, having been gone well through.   Just as
at school one wished the school-days over, though we
were happy enough there, because we expected more happiness and more liberty when we were to be our own
masters, might lie as much later in the morning as we
pleased, have no bounds and do no exercise,—just so do
I wish that my exercises were over."   At thirty-five:
" Almost the only wish I ever give utterance to is that
the next hundred years were over.   It is not that the uses
of this world seem to me weary, stale, flat, and unprofitable,—God knows far otherwise !   No man can be better
contented with his lot.   My paths are paths of pleasant-
ness. . . . .   Still the instability of human happiness is
ever before my eyes ; I long for the certain and the per-
manent."   " My notions about life are much the same as
they are about travelling—there is a good deal of amusement on the road, but, after all, one wants to be at rest."
At forty: " My disposition is invincibly cheerful, and
this alone would make me a cheerful man if I were not so
from the tenor of my life ; yet I doubt whether the
strictest Carthusian has the thought of death more habitu-
ally in his mind."

Such was Southey's constant temper ; to some persons
it may seem an unfortunate one ; to some it may be
practically unintelligible.   But those who accept of the
feast of life freely, who enter with a bounding foot its
measures of beauty and of joy,—glad to feel all the while
the serviceable sackcloth next the skin—will recognize in
Southey an instructed brother of the Renunciants' rule.

CHAPTER VI.

In October, 1805, Southey started with his friend Elmsley for a short tour in Scotland. On their way northward they stopped three days at Ashestiel. There, in a small house, rising amid its old-fashioned garden, with pastoral hills all around, and the Tweed winding at the meadow's end, lived Walter Scott. It was the year in which old Border song had waked up, with ampler echoings, in the *Lay of the Last Ministrel*, and Scott was already famous. Earlier in the year he had visited Grasmere, and had stood upon the summit of Helvellyn with Wordsworth and Davy by his side. The three October days, with their still, misty brightness, went by in full enjoyment. Southey had brought with him a manuscript containing sundry metrical romances of the fifteenth century, on which his host pored, as far as courtesy and the hours allowed, with much delight; and the guests saw Melrose, that old romance in stone so dear to Scott, went salmon-spearing on the Tweed, dined on a hare snapped up before their eyes by Percy and Douglas, and visited Yarrow. From Ashestiel they proceeded to Edinburgh. Southey looked coldly on the grey metropolis; its new city seemed a kind of Puritan Bath, which worshipped propriety instead of pleasure; but the old town seen amid the slant light of a wild red sunset

impressed him much, its vast irregular outline of roofs
and chimneys rising against tumultuous clouds like the
dismantled fragments of a giant's palace. Southey was
prepared to find himself and his friends of the Lakes persons of higher stature than the Scotch *literatuli*. Before
accepting an invitation to meet him at supper, Jeffrey
politely forwarded the proof of an unpublished review of
Madoc; if the poet preferred that his reviewer should not
present himself, Mr. Jeffrey would deny himself the pleasure of Mr. Southey's acquaintance. Southey was not to be
daunted, and, as he tells it himself, felt nothing but good-
humour on beholding a bright-faced homunculus of five-
foot-one, the centre of an attentive circle, ēēnunciating with
North-British ēēlocution his doctrines on taste. The lively
little gentleman, who thought to crush *The Excursion*—
he could as easily crush Skiddaw, said Southey—received
from the author of *Madoc* a courtesy *de haut en bas* intended to bring home to his consciousness the fact that he
was—but five-foot-one. The bland lips of the gods who
looked down on auld Reekie that evening smiled at the
magnanimity alike of poet and critic.

Two years later (1807), differences having arisen between
the proprietors and the editor of the *Edinburgh Review*, it
was in contemplation to alter the management, and Longman wrote requesting Southey to review him two or three
articles "in his best manner." Southey did not keep
firkins of criticism of first and second brand, but he was
not unwilling to receive ten guineas a sheet instead
of seven pounds. When, however, six months later,
Scott urged his friend to contribute, Judge Jeffrey still
sat on the bench of the *Edinburgh Review*, hanging,
drawing, and quartering luckless poets with undiminished
vivacity. It was of no use for Scott to assure Southey

that the homunculus, notwithstanding his flippant attacks
on *Madoc* and *Thalaba*, had the most sincere respect
for their author and his talents. Setting all personal
feelings aside, an irreconcilable difference, Southey declared, between Jeffrey and himself upon every great
principle of taste, morality, and policy, occasioned a difficulty which could not be removed. Within less than
twelve months Scott, alienated by the deepening Whiggery
of the Review, and by more personal causes, had ceased to
contribute, and opposite his name-in the list of subscribers
Constable had written, with indignant notes of exclamation, "*Stopt ! ! !*" John Murray, the young bookseller in
Fleet Street, had been to Ashestiel; in "dern privacie"
a bold complot was laid; why should the Edinburgh
clique carry it before them? The spirit of England was
still sound, and would respond to loyalty, patriotism, the
good traditions of Church and State, the temper of gentlemen, courage, scholarship; Gifford, of the Anti-Jacobin,
had surely a sturdier arm than Jeffrey; George Ellis would
remember his swashing-blow; there were the Roses, and
Matthias, and Heber; a rival Review should see the light,
and that speedily; "a good plot, good friends, and full of
expectation—an excellent plot, very good friends."

Southey was invited to write on Spanish affairs for the
first number of the *Quarterly* (Feb. 1809). His political
opinions had undergone a considerable alteration since
the days of Pantisocracy and *Joan of Arc*. The Reign of
Terror had not caused a violent reaction against the doctrine of a Republic, nor did he soon cease to sympathize
with France. But his hopes were dashed; it was plain
that "the millennium would not come this bout." Man
as he is appeared more greedy, ignorant, and dangerous
than he had appeared before, though man as he may be

was still a being composed of knowledge, virtue, and love.
The ideal republic receded into the dimness of unborn
time; no doubt—so Southey maintained to the end—a
republic is the best form of government in itself, as a sun-
dial is simpler and surer than a time-piece; but the sun of
reason does not always shine, and therefore complicated
systems of government, containing checks and counter-
checks, are needful in old countries for the present; better
systems are no doubt conceivable—for better men. "Mr.
Southey's mind," wrote Hazlitt, "is essentially sanguine,
even to over-weeningness. It is prophetic of good; it cordially embraces it; it casts a longing, lingering look after
it, even when it is gone for ever. He cannot bear to give
up the thought of happiness, his confidence in his fellow-
men, when all else despair. It is the very element 'where
he must live or have no life at all.'"   This is true;
we sacrifice too much to prudence—Southey said when
not far from sixty—and in fear of incurring the danger
or the reproach of enthusiasm, too often we stifle the
holiest impulses of the understanding and the heart.
Still at sixty he believed in a state of society actually to
be realized as superior to English society in the nineteenth century, as that itself is superior to the condition of the tattooed Britons, or of the Northern Pirates
from whom we have descended. But the error of supposing such a state of society too near, of fancying that
there is a short road to it, seemed to him a pernicious error,
seducing the young and generous into an alliance with
whatever is flagitious and detestable.

It was not until the Peace of Amiens (1802), that
Southey was restored in feeling to his own country. From
that hour the new departure in his politics may be said to
date. The honour of England became as dear to him as

to her most patriotic son; and in the man who had sub-
jugated the Swiss Republic, and thrown into a dungeon
the champion of Negro independence, and slaughtered his
prisoners at Jaffa, he indignantly refused to recognize the
representative of the generous principles of 1789. To him,
as to Wordsworth, the very life of virtue in mankind
seemed to dwell in the struggle against the military despotism which threatened to overwhelm the whole civilized
world. Whatever went along with a spirited war-policy
Southey could accept. It appeared to himself that his views
and hopes had changed precisely because the heart and soul
of his wishes had continued the same. To remove the obstacles which retard the improvement of mankind was the
one object to which, first and last, he gave his most earnest
vows. "This has been the pole-star of my course; the
needle has shifted according to the movements of the state
vessel wherein I am embarked, but the direction to which
it points has always been the same. I did not fall into the
error of those who, having been the friends of France when
they imagined that the cause of liberty was implicated in
her success, transferred their attachment from the Republic to the Military Tyranny in which it ended, and regarded
with complacency the progress of oppression because France
was the oppressor. 'They had turned their faces toward
the East in the morning to worship the rising sun, and in
the evening they were looking eastward, obstinately affirm-
ing that still the sun was there.' I, on the contrary,
altered my position as the world went round." [1]

Wordsworth has described in memorable words the
sudden exaltation of the spirit of resistance to Napoleon,
its change from the temper of fortitude to enthusiasm
animated by hope when the Spanish people rose against

_____
[1] The words quoted by Southey are his own, written in 1809.

their oppressors. "From that moment," he says, "this corruptible put on incorruption and this mortal put on immortality." Southey had learned to love the people of the Peninsula; he had almost naturalized himself among them by his studies of Spanish and Portuguese history and literature. Now there was in him a new birth of passion at a period of life when ordinarily the crust of custom begins to encase our free spirits. All his moral ardour flowed in the same current with his political enthusiasm; in this war there was as direct a contest between the principles of evil and good as the elder Persians or the Manicheans imagined in their fables. "Since the stirring day of the French Revolution," he writes to John May, "I have never felt half so much excitement in political events as the present state of Spain has given me." Little as he liked to leave home, if the Spaniards would bury their crown and sceptre, he would gird up his loins and assist at the ceremony devout as ever pilgrim at Compostella. A federal republic which should unite the peninsula and allow the internal governments to remain distinct was what Southey ardently desired. When news came of the Convention of Cintra (1808), the poet, ordinarily so punctual a sleeper, lay awake all night; since the execution of the Brissotines no public event distressed him so deeply. "How gravely and earnestly used Samuel Taylor Coleridge"—so writes Coleridge's daughter—"and William Wordsworth and my uncle Southey also to discuss the affairs of the nation, as if it all came home to their business and bosoms, as if it were their private concern! Men do not canvass these matters now-a-days, I think, quite in the same tone."

That faith in the ultimate triumph of good which sustains Southey's heroine against the persecution of the

Almighty Rajah, sustained Southey himself during the long struggle with Napoleon. A military despotism youthful and full of vigour, he said, must beat down corrupt establishments and worn-out governments, but how can it beat down for ever a true love of liberty and a true spirit of patriotism? When at last tidings reached Keswick that the Allies were in Paris, Southey's feelings were such as he had never experienced before. "The curtain had fallen after a tragedy of five-and-twenty years." The hopes and the ardours and the errors and the struggles of his early life crowded upon his mind; all things seemed to have worked together for good. He rejoiced that the whirlwind of revolution had cleared away the pestilence of the old governments; he rejoiced that right had conquered might. He did not wish to see the bad Bourbon race restored, except to complete Bonaparte's overthrow. And he feared lest an evil peace should be made. Paris taken, a commanding intellect might have cast Europe into whatever mould it pleased. "The first business," says Southey, with remarkable prevision, "should have been to have reduced France to what she was before Louis XIV.'s time; the second to have created a great power in the north of Germany with Prussia at its head; the third to have consolidated Italy into one kingdom or commonwealth."

The politicians of the *Edinburgh Review* had predicted ruin for all who dared to oppose the Corsican; they ridiculed the romantic hopes of the English nation; the fate of Spain, they declared in 1810, was decided; it would be cruel, they said, to foment petty insurrections; France had conquered Europe. It was this policy of despair which roused Scott and Southey. "We shall hoist the bloody flag," writes the latter, "down alongside

that Scotch ship, and engage her yard-arm to yard-
arm." But at first Southey, by his own request, was put
upon other work than that of firing off the heavy
Quarterly guns. Probably no man in England had read
so many books of travel; these he could review better,
he believed, than anything else; biography and history
were also within his reach; with English poetry from
Spenser onwards his acquaintance was wide and minute,
but he took no pleasure in sitting in judgment on his
contemporaries; his knowledge of the literary history of
Spain and Portugal was a speciality, which, as often as
the readers of the Review could bear with it, might be
brought into use. Two things he could promise without
fail—perfect sincerity in what he might write, without the
slightest pretension of knowledge which he did not possess,
and a punctuality not to be exceeded by Mr. Murray's
opposite neighbour, the clock of St. Dunstan's.

Southey's essays, literary, biographical, historical, and
miscellaneous, would probably now exist in a collected
form, and constitute a storehouse of information,—information often obtained with difficulty, and always conveyed
in a lucid and happy style,—were it not that he chose
on the eve of the Reform Bill to earn whatever unpopu-
larity he could by collecting his essays on political and
social subjects. Affairs had hurried forward with eager
strides; these *Quarterly* articles seemed already far behind,
and might safely be left to take a quiet corner in Time's
wallet among the alms for oblivion. Yet Southey's
political articles had been effective in their day, and
have still a value by no means wholly antiquarian. His
home politics had been in the main determined by his
convictions on the great European questions. There was
a party of revolution in this country eager to break with

the past, ready to venture every experiment for a future
of mere surmise. Southey believed that the moral sense
of the English people, their regard for conduct, would
do much to preserve them from lawless excess; still,
the lesson read by recent history was that order once
overthrown, anarchy follows, to be itself quelled by
the lordship of the sword. Rights, however, were pleaded
—shall we refuse to any man the rights of a man ?
"Therapeutics," says Southey, "were in a miserable
state as long as practitioners proceeded upon the gra-
tuitous theory of elementary complexions; . . . . natural
philosophy was no better, being a mere farrago of romance,
founded upon idle tales or fanciful conjectures, not upon
observation and experiment. The science of politics is
just now in the same stage; it has been erected by
shallow sophists upon abstract rights and imaginary
compacts, without the slightest reference to habits and
history." "Order and improvement" were the words
inscribed on Southey's banner. Order, that England
might not fall, as France had fallen, into the hands of a
military saviour of society ; order, that she might be
in a condition to wage her great feud on behalf of freedom
with undivided energy. Order, therefore, first; not by
repression alone—though there were a time and a place
for repression also—but order with improvement as a
portion of its very life and being. Southey was a poet
and a moralist, and judged of the well-being of a people
by other than material standards ; the wealth of nations
seemed to him something other and higher than can be ascer-
tained by wages and prices, rent and revenue, exports
and imports. "True it is," he writes, "the ground is more
highly cultivated, the crooked hedgerows have been thrown
down, the fields are in better shape and of handsomer

dimensions, the plough makes longer furrows, there is more
corn and fewer weeds ; but look at the noblest produce of
the earth, look at the children of the soil, look at the seeds
which are sown here for immortality !" "The system
which produces the happiest moral effects will be found
the most beneficial to the interest of the individual and
the general weal ; upon this basis the science of political
economy will rest at last, when the ponderous volumes
with which it has been overlaid shall have sunk by their
own weight into the dead sea of oblivion." Looking
about him he asked, What do the English people chiefly
need? More wealth ? It may be so ; but rather wisdom
to use the wealth they have. More votes ? Yes, hereafter ;
but first the light of knowledge, that men may see
how to use a vote. Even the visible beauty and grace
of life seemed to Southey a precious thing, the loss of
which might be set over against some gain in pounds,
shillings, and pence. The bleak walls and barrack-like
windows of a manufactory, the long unlovely row of
operatives' dwellings, struck a chill into his heart. He
contrasts the old cottages substantially built of native
stone, mellowed by time, taken by nature to herself with a
mother's fondness, the rose-bushes beside the door, the
little patch of flower-garden—he contrasts these with the
bald deformities in which the hands of a great mill are
stalled.

Before all else national education appeared to Southey
to be the need of England. He saw a great population
growing up with eager appetites, and consciousness of
augmented power. Whence were moral thoughtfulness
and self-restraint to come ? Not surely from the triumph
of liberal opinions ; not from the power to read every
incentive to vice and sedition ; nor from Religious Tract

Societies; nor from the portentous bibliolatry of the
Evangelical party.   But there is an education which
at once enlightens the understanding and trains the conscience and the will.   And there is that great association
for making men good, the Church of England.   Connect
the two,—education and the Church; the progress of
enlightenment, virtue, and piety however gradual will
be sure.   Subordinate to this primary measure of reform,
national education, many other measures were advocated
by Southey.   He looked forward to a time when, the great
struggle respecting property over—for this struggle he saw
looming not far off—public opinion will no more tolerate
the extreme of poverty in a large class of the people than
it now tolerates slavery in Europe; when the aggregation
of land in the hands of great owners must cease, when
that community of lands, which Owen of Lanark would
too soon anticipate, might actually be realized.   But these
things were perhaps far off.   Meanwhile how to bring
nearer the golden age?   Southey's son has made out a
long list of the measures urged upon the English people
in the *Quarterly Review*, or elsewhere, by his father.
Bearing in mind that the proposer of these measures
resisted the Reform Bill, Free Trade, and Catholic Emancipation, any one curious in such things may determine
with what political label he should be designated:—
National education; the diffusion of cheap and good
literature; a well-organized system of colonization, and
especially of female emigration;[2] a wholesome training

[2] " With the Cape and New Holland I would proceed thus:—
' Govern yourselves, and we will protect you as long as you need
protection; when that is no longer necessary, remember that
though we be different countries, each independent, we are one
people.' "—R. S. to W. S. Landor.   Letters, vol ii. p. 263.

for the children of misery and vice in great cities; the
establishment of Protestant sisters of charity and a better
order of hospital nurses; the establishment of savings'
banks in all small towns; the abolition of flogging in the
army and navy, except in extreme cases; improvements
in the poor laws; alterations in the game laws; alterations
in the criminal laws, as inflicting the punishment of death
in far too many cases; execution of criminals within
prison walls; alterations in the factory system for the
benefit of the operative, and especially as to the employment of children; national works—reproductive if possible—to be undertaken in times of peculiar distress; the
necessity of doing away with interments in crowded cities;
the system of giving allotments of ground to labourers;
the employment of paupers in cultivating waste lands;
the commutation of tithes; and last, the need for more
clergymen, more colleges, more courts of law.

"Mr. Southey," said Hazlitt, "missed his way in
Utopia; he has found it at old Sarum." He found it in
England, in the State, and in the Church, with its ordered
freedom, its serious aspiration, its habitual pieties, its
reasonable service, its reverent history, its beauty of
holiness, its close where priests, who are husbands and
fathers, live out their calm benignant lives, its amiable
home for those whose toil is ended and who now sleep
well. But how Southey found his way from his early
deism to Anglican orthodoxy cannot be precisely determined. Certainly not for many years could he have made
that subscription to the Articles of the Church of England,
which at the first barred his way to taking orders. The
superstition, which seemed to be the chief spiritual food
of Spain, had left Southey for the rest of his life a resolute
opponent of Catholicism; and as he read lives of the Saints

and histories of the Orders, the exclamation " I do well to
be angry" was often on his lips. For the wisdom, learning, and devotion of the Jesuits he had, however, a just
respect. Geneva, with its grim logic and stark spirituality,
suited nerves of a different temper from his. For a
time Southey thought himself half a Quaker, but he
desired more visible beauty, and more historical charm
than he could find in Quakerism. Needing a comely
home for his spiritual affections, he found precisely what
pleased him built in the pleasant Anglican close. With
growing loyalty to the State, his loyalty to the Church
could not but keep pace. He loved her tolerance, her
culture ; he fed upon her judicious and learned writers ;—
Taylor, with his bright fancies like the little rings of
the vine ; South, hitting out straight from the shoulder
at anarchy, fanaticism, and licentiousness, as Southey
himself would have liked to hit ; Jackson, whose weight
of character made his pages precious as with golden
bullion. After all, old England had some advantages
over Utopia.

The English Constitution consisting of Church and State,
it seemed to Southey an absurdity in politics to give those
persons power in the State whose duty it is to subvert the
Church. Admit Catholics, he said, to every office of trust,
emolument, or honour ; only never admit them into Parliament. " The arguments about equal rights are fit only
for a schoolboy's declamation ; it may as well be said that
the Jew has a right to be a bishop, or the Quaker an
admiral, as that the Roman Catholic has a right to a seat
in the British Legislature ; his opinions disqualify him."
To call this a question of toleration was impudence;
Catholics were free to practise the rites of their religion ;
they had the full and free use of the press ; perfect tolera-

tion was granted to the members of that church, which, wherever dominant, tolerates no other.   Catholic Emancipation would not conciliate Ireland ; the great source of Irish misery had been not England's power, but her weakness, and those violences to which weakness resorts in self-defence ; old sores were not to be healed by the admission of Catholic demagogues into Parliament.   The measure styled Emancipation would assuredly be followed by the downfall of the Protestant Establishment in Ireland, and by the spread of Catholicism in English society.   To Pyrrhonists one form of faith might seem as good or as bad as the other ; but the great mass of the English people had not advanced so far in the march of intellect as to perceive no important difference between Catholic and Protestant doctrine, or between Catholic and Protestant morality.   By every possible means better the condition of the Irish peasantry ; give them employment in public works ; facilitate, for those who desire it, the means of emigration ; extend the poor-laws to Ireland, and lay that impost on absentees in such a proportion as may compensate in some degree for their non-residence ; educate the people ; execute justice and maintain peace, and the cry of Catholic Emancipation may be safely disregarded.

So Southey pleaded in the *Quarterly Review*.   With reference to Emancipation and to the Reform Bill he and Wordsworth, who perhaps had not kept themselves sufficiently in relation with living men and the public sentiment of the day, were in their solitude gifted with a measure of the prophetic spirit, which in some degree explains their alarms.   For the prophet who knows little of expediency and nothing of the manipulation of parties, nothing of the tangled skein of contending interests, sees the future in its moral causes, and he sees it in a vision. But he cannot date the appearances in his vision. Battle, and garments rolled in blood, and trouble, and dimness of anguish pass before him, and he proclaims what it is given him to see. It matters not a little, however, in the actual event, whether the battle be on the morrow or half a century hence; and the prophet furnishes us with no chronology, or at best with some vague time and times and half a time. New forces have arisen before the terrors of his prediction come to pass, and therefore when they come to pass their effect is often altogether different from that anticipated. Wordsworth and Southey were right in declaring that a vast and formidable change was taking place in the England of their day; many things which they, amid incredulous scoffs, announced have become actual; others remain to be fulfilled. But the events have taken up their place in an order of things foreign to the conceptions of the prophets; the fire from heaven descends, but meanwhile we, ingenious sons of men, have set up a lightning-conductor.

Southey and the *Quarterly Review* were often spoken of as a single entity. But the Review in truth never precisely represented his feelings and convictions. With Gifford he had no literary sympathies. Gifford's heart was full of kindness, says Southey, for all living creatures except authors; *them* he regarded as Isaac Walton did the worm. Against the indulgence of that temper Southey always protested; yet he was chosen to bear the reproach of having tortured Keats, and of having anonymously glorified himself at the expense of Shelley. Gifford's omissions, additions, substitutions, often caused Southey's article in the Review to be very unlike the article which he had despatched to the editor in manuscript. Probably these changes were often made on

warrantable grounds. Southey's confidence in his own
opinions, which always seemed to him to be based upon
moral principles, was high ; and he was not in the habit of
diluting his ink. Phrases which sounded well in the
library of Greta Hall had quite another sound in Mr.
Murray's office in Fleet Street.

On arriving in London for a short visit in the autumn
of 1813, Southey learnt that the Prince Regent wished
to confer on him the Laureateship vacant by the death
of Pye. Without consulting the Regent, Lord Liverpool had previously directed that the office should be
offered to Walter Scott. On the moment came a letter
from Scott informing Southey that he had declined the
appointment, not from any foolish prejudice against holding it, but because he was already provided for, and would
not engross emoluments which ought to be awarded to a
man of letters who had no other views in life. Southey hesi-
tated, having ceased for several years to produce occasional
verses; but his friend Croker assured him that he would
not be compelled to write odes as boys write exercises
at stated times on stated subjects, that it would suffice
if he wrote on great public events, or did not write,
as the spirit moved him, and thus his scruples were
overcome. In a little, low, dark room in the purlieus
of St. James',—a solitary clerk being witness—the oath
was duly administered by a fat old gentleman-usher
in full buckle, Robert Southey swearing to be a faithful servant to the King, to reveal all treasons which
might come to his knowledge, and to obey the Lord
Chamberlain in all matters of the King's service. It was
Scott's belief that his generosity had provided for his poorer
brother bard an income of three or four hundred pounds a
year. In reality the emolument was smaller and the task-

work more irksome than had been supposed. The tierce
of Canary swilled by Ben Jonson and his poetic sons,
had been wickedly commuted for a small sum ; the whole
net-income amounted to 90*l*. But this, " the very least
of Providence's mercies," as a poor clergyman said when
pronouncing grace over a herring, secured an important
happiness for Southey ; he did not employ it, as Byron
puts it, to butter his bread on both sides ; he added twelve
pounds to it and vested it forthwith in an insurance upon
his own life. " I have never felt any painful anxiety
about providing for my family . . ." he writes to Scott,
" but it is with the deepest feeling of thanksgiving that
I have secured this legacy for my wife and children, and
it is to you that I am primarily and chiefly indebted."

Croker's assurance was too hastily given. The birthday Ode indeed fell into abeyance during the long malady
of George III., but the New Year's Ode had still to be
provided. Southey was fortunate in 1814 ; events worthy
of celebration had taken place ; a dithyramb or rather an
oration in lines of irregular length was accordingly
produced ; and was forwarded to his musical yoke-fellow
Sir William Parsons. But the sight of Southey's page,
over which the longs and shorts meandered seemingly at
their own sweet will, shocked the orderly mind of the chief
musician. What kind of ear could Mr. Southey have ?
His predecessor, the lamented Mr. Pye, had written his
Odes always in regular stanzas. What kind of action was
this exhibited by the unbroken State Pegasus ? Duly as
each New Year approached Southey set himself to what he
called his *ode*ous job ; it was the price he paid for the
future comfort of his children. While his political
assailants pictured the author of *Joan of Arc* as a court-
lacquey following in the train of the fat Adonis, he with

grim cheerfulness was earning a provision for his girls, and had it not been a duty to kiss hands on the appointment, His Royal Highness the Prince Regent would never have seen his poet. Gradually the New Year's Ode ceased to be looked for, and Southey was emancipated. His verse-making as laureate occasionally rose into something higher than journeyman work; when public events stirred his heart to joy or grief, or indignation, he wrote many admirable periods of measured rhetoric. *The Funeral Song for the Princess Charlotte* is of a higher strain; a knell, heavy yet clear-toned, is tolled by its finely wrought octosyllabics.

A few months after the battle of Waterloo, which had so deeply moved Southey, he started with his wife, a rare voyager from Keswick, and his little daughter Edith May, on a pilgrimage to the scene of victory. The aunts remained to take care of Bertha, Kate, and Isabel, with the nine-years-old darling of all, the only boy, Herbert. With Bruges, "like a city of Elizabeth's age—you expect to see a head with a ruff looking from the window," Southey was beyond measure delighted. At Ghent he ransacked bookshops, and was pleased to see in the Beguinage the realization of his own and Rickman's ideas on Sisterhoods. On a clear September day the travellers visited the battlefield; the autumnal sunshine with soft airs, and now and again a falling leaf, while the bees were busy among the year's last flowers, suited well with the poet's mood of thankfulness tempered by solemn thought. When early in December they returned with a lading of toys to their beloved lake-country, little Edith had hardly recovered from an illness which had attacked her at Aix. It was seven o'clock in the evening by the time they reached Rydal, and to press forward and arrive

M

while the children were asleep would be to defraud every-
one of the first reward earned by so long absence. "A
return home under fortunate circumstances has something
of the character of a triumph and requires daylight." The
glorious presence of Skiddaw, and Derwent bright under
the winter sky, asked also for a greeting at noon rather
than at night. A depth of grave and tender thankfulness
lay below Southey's joy that morning; it was twelve years
since he had pitched his tent here beside the Greta;
twelve years had made him feel the touch of time; but
what blessings they had brought: all his heart's desire was
here—books, children, leisure, and a peace that passeth
understanding. The instant hour, however, was not for
meditation but for triumph :—

> O joyful hour, when to our longing home
>   The long-expected wheels at length drew nigh!
> When the first sound went forth, " they come! they come!"
>   And hope's impatience quicken'd every eye!
> " Never had man whom Heaven would heap with bliss
> More glad return, more happy hour than this."
>
> Aloft on yonder bench, with arms dispread,
>   My boy stood, shouting there his father's name,
> Waving his hat around his happy head;
>   And there a younger group his sisters came:
> Smiling they stood with looks of pleased surprise
> While tears of joy were seen in elder eyes.
>
> Soon all and each came crowding round to share
>   The cordial greeting, the beloved sight;
> What welcomings of hand and lip were there!
>   And when those overflowings of delight
> Subsided to a sense of quiet bliss,
> Life hath no purer, deeper happiness.
>
> The young companion of our weary way
>   Found here the end desired of all her ills;
> She who in sickness pining many a day
>   Hunger'd and thirsted for her native hills,

Forgetful now of suffering past and pain,
Rejoiced to see her own dear home again.

Recovered now the homesick mountaineer
   Sate by the playmate of her infancy,
The twin-like comrade,[3]—render'd doubly dear
   For that long absence; full of life was she
With voluble discourse and eager mien
Telling of all the wonders she had seen.

Here silently between her parents stood
   My dark-eyed Bertha, timid as a dove;
And gently oft from time to time she woo'd
   Pressure of hand, or word, or look of love,
With impulse shy of bashful tenderness,
Soliciting again the wished caress.

The younger twain in wonder lost were they,
   My gentle Kate and my sweet Isabel:
Long of our promised coming, day by day,
   It had been their delight to hear and tell;
And now when that long-promised hour was come,
Surprise and wakening memory held them dumb.

      *   *   *   *   *

Soon they grew blithe as they were wont to be;
   Her old endearments each began to seek;
And Isabel drew near to climb my knee,
   And pat with fondling hand her father's cheek;
With voice and touch and look reviving thus
The feelings which had slept in long disuse.

But there stood one whose heart could entertain
   And comprehend the fulness of the joy;
The father, teacher, playmate, was again
   Come to his only and his studious boy;
And he beheld again that mother's eye
Which with such ceaseless care had watched his infancy.

---

[3] Sara Coleridge.

Bring forth the treasures now,—a proud display,—
  For rich as Eastern merchants we return !
Behold the black Beguine, the Sister grey,
  The Friars whose heads with sober motion turn,
The Ark well-filled with all its numerous hives,
Noah and Shem and Ham and Japhet and their wives.

The tumbler loose of limb; the wrestlers twain ;
  And many a toy beside of quaint device,
Which, when his fleecy flocks no more can gain
  Their pasture on the mountains hoar with ice,
The German shepherd carves with curious knife,
Earning in easy toil the food of frugal life.

It was a group which Richter had he viewed,
  Might have deemed worthy of his perfect skill ;
The keen impatience of the younger brood,
  Their eager eyes and fingers never still ;
The hope, the wonder, and the restless joy
Of those glad girls and that vociferous boy.

The aged friend [4] serene with quiet smile,
  Who in their pleasure finds her own delight ;
The mother's heart-felt happiness the while ;
  The aunts' rejoicing in the joyful sight ;
And he who in his gaiety of heart,
With glib and noisy tongue performed the showman's part.

It was manifest to a thoughtful observer, says De
Quincey, that Southey's golden equanimity was bound up
in a trinity of chords, a three-fold chain—in a conscience
clear of offence, in the recurring enjoyments from his
honourable industry, and in the gratification of his parental
affections. In the light of Herbert's smiles his father
almost lived, the very pulses of his heart played in unison
with the sound of his son's laughter. "There was," De
Quincey goes on, "in his manner towards this child, and
towards this only, something that marked an excess of

[4] Mrs. Wilson—then aged seventy-two.

delirious doating, perfectly unlike the ordinary chastened movement of Southey's affections; and something also which indicated a vague fear about him; a premature unhappiness as if already the inaudible tread of calamity could be divined, as if already he had lost him." As a baby, while Edith was only "like an old book ugly and good," Herbert, in spite of his Tartar eyes, a characteristic of Southey babyhood, was already beautiful. At six he was more gentle and more loving, says Southey, than you can almost conceive. "He has just learnt his Greek alphabet, and is so desirous of learning, so attentive and so quick of apprehension, that if it please God he should live, there is little doubt but that something will come out of him." In April, 1809, Southey writes to Landor twenty-four hours after an attack of croup which seized his boy had been subdued: "Even now I am far, very far from being at ease. There is a love which passeth the love of women, and which is more lightly alarmed than the lightest jealousy. Landor, I am not a Stoic at home; I feel as you do about the fall of an old tree! but, O Christ! what a pang it is to look upon the young shoot and think it will be cut down. And this is the thought which almost at all times haunts me; it comes upon me in moments when I know not whether the tears that start are of love or of bitterness."

The alarm of 1809 passed away, and Herbert grew to the age of nine, active and bright of spirit, yet too pale and, like his father, hanging too constantly over his books; a finely organized being, delicate in his sensibilities and prematurely accomplished. Before the snow had melted which shone on Skiddaw that day when the children welcomed home their parents, Herbert Southey lay in his grave. His disease was an affection of the heart, and for

weeks his father, palsied by apprehension, and unable to put
hand to his regular work, stood by the bedside, with composed countenance, with words of hope, and agonized
heart.   Each day of trial made his boy more dear.   With
a trembling pride Southey saw the sufferer's behaviour,
beautiful in this illness as in all his life ; nothing could
be more calm, more patient, more collected, more dutiful,
more admirable.   At last, worn with watching, Southey
and his wife were prevailed upon to lie down.   The good
Mary Barker watched, and it is she who writes the
following lines :—" Herbert !—that sweetest and most
perfect of all children on this earth, who died in my
arms at nine years of age, whose death I announced
to his father and mother in their bed, where I had prayed
and persuaded them to go.   When Southey could speak, his
first words were, ' *The Lord hath given, and the Lord hath
taken away.   Blessed be the name of the Lord !*'   Never
can I forget that moment " (1816).

"I am perfectly resigned," Southey wrote to Bedford
on the most mournful of all days, "and do not give way
to grief.   Thank God I can control myself for the sake of
others."   But next morning found him weak as a child,
even weaker in body than in mind, for long anxiety
had worn him to the bone, and while he tried to calm
and console the rest, his limbs trembled under him.   His
first wild wish to fly from Keswick passed away ; it was
good to be there near the boy's grave.   Weak as he was,
he flung himself upon his work.   "I employ myself
incessantly, taking, however, every day as much exercise
as I can bear without injurious fatigue, which is not
much."   "It would surprise you were you to see what
I get through in a day."   "For the first week I did
as much every day as would at other times have seemed

the full and overflowing produce of three." From his
early discipline in the stoical philosophy some help
now was gained; from his active and elastic mind the
gain was more; but these would have been insufficient
to support him without a heart-felt and ever-present
faith that what he had lost was not lost for ever. A
great change had indeed come upon him. He set his
house in order, and made arrangements as if his own
death were at hand. He resolved not to be unhappy,
but the joyousness of his disposition had received its
death-wound; he felt as if he had passed at once from
boyhood to the decline of life. He tried dutifully to
make head against his depression, but at times with
poor success. "I employ myself, and have recovered
strength, but in point of spirits I rather lose ground."
Still there are hidden springs of comfort. "The head
and flower of my earthly happiness is cut off. But
I am *not* unhappy." "When I give way to tears,
which is only in darkness or solitude, they are not tears
of unmingled pain." All beloved ones grew more precious; the noble fortitude of his wife made her more
than ever a portion of his best self. His uncle's boy,
Edward, he could not love more than he had loved him
before; but, "as far as possible, he will be to me hereafter," writes Southey, "in the place of my son." And
in truth the blessing of Herbert's boyhood remained with
him still; a most happy, a most beautiful boyhood it
had been; he was thankful for having possessed the child
so long; "for worlds I would not but have been his
father." "I have abundant blessings left; for each and
all of these I am truly thankful; but of all the blessings
which God has given me, this child, who is removed, is
the one I *still* prize the most." To relieve feelings which

he dared not utter with his lips, he thought of setting
about a monument in verse for Herbert and himself, which
might make one inseparable memory for father and son.
A page or two of fragmentary thoughts in verse and prose
for this poetic monument exists, but Southey could not
keep his imagination enough above his heart to dare to go
on with it ; to do so would have dissolved his heart anew.
One or two of these holy scriptures of woe, truly red drops
of Southey's life-blood, will tell enough of this love passing
the love of women.

Thy life was a day, and sum it well, life is but a week of such
days,—with how much storm and cold and darkness! Thine was
a sweet spring day—a vernal Sabbath, all sunshine, hope, and
promise.

---

and that name
In sacred silence buried, which was still
At morn and eve the never-wearying theme
Of dear discourse.

---

playful thoughts
Turned now to gall and esil.

No more great attempts, only a few autumnal flowers like second
primroses, &c.

They who look for me in our Father's kingdom
Will look for him also ; inseparably
Shall we be remembered.

Come then
Pain and Infirmity—appointed guests,
My heart is ready.

From the day of his son's death Southey began to step

down from the heights of life, with a steadfast foot, and
head still held erect. He recovered cheerfulness, but it
was as one who has undergone an amputation seeks
the sunshine. Herbert's grave anchored him in Keswick. An offer of two thousand pounds a year for a daily
article in the *Times* did not tempt him to London.
His home, his books, his literary work, Skiddaw, Derwentwater, and Crosthwaite churchyard were too dear.
Three years later came the unlooked-for birth of a second
boy ; and Cuthbert was loved by his father ; but the love
was chastened and controlled, of autumnal beauty and
seriousness.

When the war with France had ended, depression
of trade was acutely felt in England ; party spirit ran
high, and popular passions were dangerously roused. In
the spring of 1817, the Laureate saw to his astonishment
a poem entitled *Wat Tyler* by Robert Southey advertised
as just published. He had written this lively dramatic
sketch in the full fervour of Republicanism twenty-three
years previously ; the manuscript had passed into other
hands, and he had long ceased to think of it. The skulk-
ing rogue and the knavish publisher who now gave it to
the world had chosen their time judiciously ; this rebuke
to the apostate of the *Quarterly* would be a sweet morsel
for gossip-mongers to roll under the tongue, an infallible
pill to purge melancholy with all true children of progress.
No fewer than sixty thousand copies, it is said, were sold.
Wat Tyler suited well with Southey's nonage ; it has a
bright rhetorical fierceness of humanity. The speech-
making radical blacksmith, " still toiling yet still poor,"
his insulted daughter, her virtuous lover, the communist
priest John Ball, whose amiable theology might be that
of Mr. Belsham in his later days, stand over against the

tyrant king, his Archiepiscopal absolver from oaths, the
haughty nobles, and the servile minions of the law. There
was nothing in the poem that could be remembered with
shame, unless it is shameful to be generous and inexperienced at the age of twenty. But England in 1817
seemed charged with combustibles, and even so small a
spark as this was not to be blown about without a care.
The Prince Regent had been fired at ; there were com-
mittals for treason ; there were riots in Somersetshire ;
the swarm of Manchester Blanketeers announced a march
to London ; the Habeas Corpus was suspended ; before
the year was out, Brandreth and his fellows had been
executed at Derby. Southey applied to the Court
of Chancery for an injunction to restrain the publication of his poem. It was refused by Lord Eldon
on the ground that the publication being one calculated
to do injury to society, the author could not reclaim his
property in it. There the matter might have dropped ; but
it seemed good to Mr. William Smith representing liberal
Norwich, where Southey had many friends, to take his
seat in the House of Commons one evening with the
Quarterly Review in one pocket and *Wat Tyler* in the
other, and to read aloud contrasted extracts showing how
the malignant renegade could play the parts, as it suited
him, of a seditious firebrand and a servile courtier. Wynn
on the spot administered a well-deserved rebuke ; Wilber-
force wrote to Southey that had he been present, his voice
would also have been heard ; Coleridge vindicated him in
the *Courier.* Seldom indeed was Southey drawn into con-
troversy. When pelted with abuse he walked on with
uplifted head, and did not turn round ; it seemed to him
that he was of a stature to invite bespattering. His self-
confidence was high and calm ; that he possessed no com-

mon abilities was certain: and the amount of toil which
went into his books gave him a continual assurance of
their worth which nothing could gainsay ; he had no time
for moods of dejection and self-distrust.   But if Southey
struck he struck with force, and tried to leave his mark
on his antagonist.   To repel this attack made in the
House of Commons was a duty.   *A Letter to William
Smith, Esq., M.P.,* was written, as Wordsworth wished,
with the strength of masculine indignation ; blow after
blow is planted with sure effect ; no word is wasted ;
there is skill in the hard hitting ; and the antagonist
fairly overthrown, Southey, with one glance of scorn,
turns on his heel, and moves lightly away.   " I wish you
joy," wrote Walter Scott, "of your triumphant answer.
. . . . Enough of this gentleman, who I think will not
walk out of the round again to slander the conduct of
individuals."   The concluding sentences of the Letter
give in brief Southey's fearless review of his unstained
career.

How far the writings of Mr. Southey may be found to deserve
a favourable acceptance from after ages, time will decide; but a
name which, whether worthily or not, has been conspicuous in
the literary history of its age, will certainly not perish. . . . .
It will be related that he lived in the bosom of his family, in
absolute retirement; that in all his writings there breathed the
same abhorrence of oppression and immorality, the same spirit
of devotion, and the same ardent wishes for the melioration of
mankind : and that the only charge which malice could bring
against him was, that as he grew older, his opinions altered concerning the means by which that melioration was to be effected,
and that as he learnt to understand the institutions of his
country, he learnt to appreciate them rightly, to love, and to
revere, and to defend them.   It will be said of him, that in an
age of personality he abstained from satire ; and that during
the course of his literary life, often as he was assailed, the only

occasion on which he ever condescended to reply, was, when a
certain Mr. William Smith insulted him in Parliament with the
appellation of renegade.   On that occasion, it will be said, he
vindicated himself, as it became him to do, and treated his
calumniator with just and memorable severity.   Whether it
shall be added, that Mr. William Smith redeemed his own
character by coming forward with honest manliness, and ac-
knowledging that he had spoken rashly and unjustly, concerns
himself, but is not of the slightest importance to me.

One other personal strife is worthy of notice.   When
visiting London in 1813, he made the acquaintance of
Byron.   "Is Southey magnanimous ?"   Byron asked Rogers,
remembering how he had tried his wit in early days on
Thalaba and *Madoc*.   Rogers could answer for Southey's
magnanimity, and the two poets met, Southey finding in
Byron very much more to like than he had expected, and
Byron being greatly struck by Southey's " epic appearance."   " To have that poet's head and shoulders," he
said, " I would almost have written his Sapphics."   And
in his diary he wrote : " Southey's talents are of the first
order.   His prose is perfect. . . .   He has probably written
too much of poetry for the present generation ; posterity
will probably select; but he has passages equal to anything."   At a later date Byron thought Southey's *Roderick*
" the first poem of the time."   But when about to publish *Don Juan*, a work " too free for these very modest
days," what better mode of saucily meeting public opinion,
and getting a first laugh on his side, than to dedicate such
a poem to a virtuous Laureate, and show that he and his
fellows who had uttered nothing base, were yet political
turncoats, not entitled by any superfine morality to as-
sume airs of indignation against him and his reprobate
hero ?   The dedication was shown about and laughed
over, though not yet printed.   Southey heard of these

things and felt released from that restraint of good feeling which made him deal tenderly in his writings with every one to whom he had once given his hand. An attack upon himself would not alone have roused Southey ; no man received abuse with more self-possession. Political antagonism would still have left him able to meet a fellow-poet on the common ground of literature. When distress fastened upon Leigh Hunt, whose *Examiner* and *Liberal* had never spared the Laureate, Mr. Forster did not hesitate to apply to Southey for assistance, which was declined solely because the circular put forward Leigh Hunt's political services as those chiefly entitling him to relief. " Those who are acquainted with me," Southey wrote, "know that I am neither resentful nor intolerant," and after expressing admiration of Leigh Hunt's powers, the letter goes on to suggest that his friends should draw up a circular in which, without compromising any of his opinions, the appeal might be made solely upon the score of literary merit, " placing him thus, as it were, within the sacred territory which ought always to be considered and respected as neutral ground." Wise and admirable words ! But there was one offence which was to Southey the unforgiveable sin against the holy spirit of a nation's literature. To entice poetry from the altar, and to degrade her for the pleasure of wanton imaginations seemed to Southey, feeling as he did the sanctity of the love of husband and wife, of father and child, to be treason against humanity. Southey was indeed tolerant of a certain Rabelaisian freedom in playing with some of the enclosed incidents of our life. " All the greatest of poets," he says, "have had a spice of Pantagruelism in their composition, which I verily believe was essential to their greatness." But to take an extravagant fling in costume of a *sans-culotte*, and

to play the part of " pander-general to the youth of Great
Britain," were different things. In his preface to *A Vision
of Judgment*, Southey deplored the recent fall in the ethical
spirit of English literature, " which for half a century had
been distinguished for its moral purity," and much of the
guilt he laid on the leaders of " the Satanic School." In
the long run the interests of art, as of all high endeavour, are
invariably proved to be one with the interest of a nation's
morality. It had taken many lives of men to lift literature
out of the beast. From prudential virtue and the lighter
ethics of Addison it had risen to the grave moral dignity of
Johnson, and from that to the impassioned spirituality of
Wordsworth. Should all this be abandoned, and should
literature now be permitted to reel back into the brute ?
We know that the title " Satanic School " struck home,
that Byron was moved, and replied with brilliant play of
wit in his *Vision of Judgment*. The laughers went over to
Byron's side. One who would be witty has certain advantages, if content to disregard honesty and good manners.
To be witty was not Southey's concern. " I saw," he said
many years after, " that Byron was a man of quick impulses, strong passions, and great powers. I saw him abuse
these powers; and, looking at the effect of his writings
on the public mind, it was my duty to denounce such of
them as aimed at the injury of morals and religion. This
was all." If continental critics find in what he set down
a characteristic example of the bourgeois morality of
England, we note with interest their point of view.[5]

"Bertha, Kate, and Isabel," wrote Southey on June 26,
1820, " you have been very good girls, and have written

[5] To certain false allegations of fact made by Byron, Southey
replied in *The Courier*, and reprinted his letters in *Essays, Moral
and Political*, vol. ii. pp. 183—205.

me very nice letters, with which I was much pleased. This
is the last letter which I can write in return ; and as I
happen to have a quiet hour to myself here at Streatham,
on Monday noon, I will employ that hour in relating to
you the whole history and manner of my being ell-ell-
deed at Oxford, by the Vice-Chancellor." Public dis-
tinctions of this kind he rated perhaps below their true
value. To stand well with Murray and Longman was more
to him than any handle to his name. A similar honour
from Cambridge he declined. His gold medal from the
Royal Society of Literature he changed for a silver coffee-pot
for Mrs. Southey. To " be be-doctored and called everything that ends in issimus," was neither any harm nor
much good ; but to take his seat between such doctors as
the Duke of Wellington, and—perhaps—Sir Walter Scott
was a temptation. When his old school-fellow Phillimore
presented Southey, the theatre rang with applause. Yet
the day was indeed one of the heaviest in his life. Never
had he stopped for a night in Oxford since he left it in
1794, intending to bid farewell to Europe for an Utopia
in some back settlement of America. Not one who
really loved him—for Scott could not appear—was
present. When in the morning he went to look at
Balliol, no one remembered him except old Adams, who
had attempted to dress his hair as a freshman, and old
Mrs. Adams, the laundress, both now infirm. From the
tumultuous theatre Southey strolled into Christ Church
walks alone. What changes time had made ! Many of the
friends with whom he had sauntered there were in their
graves. So brooding he chewed the bitter-sweet of remembrance, until at length a serious gratitude prevailed.
" Little girls," the letter ends, " you know it might be
proper for me now to wear a large wig, and to be called

Doctor Southey, and to become very severe, and leave off
being a comical papa. And if you should find that ell-ell-
deeing has made this difference in me, you will not be surprised. However, I shall not come down in my wig,
neither shall I wear my robes at home."

While in Holland in the summer of 1826, a more conspicuous honour was unexpectedly thrust upon Southey.
The previous year he had gone abroad with Henry Taylor, and at Douay was bitten on the foot by Satan,
according to his conjecture, sitting squat at his great toe ;
at Leyden he was obliged to rest his inflamed foot, and
there it was his good fortune to be received into the house
of the poet Bilderdijk, a delightful old erudite and enthusiast, whose charming wife was the translator of *Roderick*.
In 1826 he visited his kind friends once more, and at
Brussels received the surprising intelligence that during
his absence he had been elected a member of Parliament.
Lord Radnor, an entire stranger, had read with admiration
Southey's confession of faith concerning Church and
State, in the last paragraph of his *Book of the Church*.
By his influence the poet had been elected for the borough
of Downton ; the return, however, was null, for Southey
held a pension during pleasure, and, even if this were
resigned, where was the property qualification? This
latter objection was met by Sir Robert Inglis, who
desired to know whether Southey would sit in Parliament
if an estate of 300*l.* a year were purchased for him. An
estate of 300*l.* a year would be a very agreeable thing to
Robert Lackland ; but he had no mind to enter on a new
public sphere for which he was ill qualified by his previous life, to risk the loss of health by midnight debates,
to abandon the education of his little boy, and to separate
himself more or less from his wife and daughters. He

could not be wrong, he believed, in the quiet confidence
which assured him that he was in his proper place.

Now more than ever before Edith Southey needed her
husband's sustaining love. On the day of his return to
Keswick, while amused to find himself the object of mob
popularity, he learnt that one of his daughters was ailing ;
the illness, however, already seemed to have passed the
worst. This appearance of amendment quickly proved
deceptive; and on a Sunday evening in mid July, Isabel,
"the most radiant creature that I ever beheld or shall behold," passed away, while her father was on his knees in
the room below, praying that she might be released from
suffering either by recovery or by death. All that had
been gone through ten years before, renewed itself with
dread exactness. Now as then the first day was one of
stunned insensibility ; now as then the next morning found
him weak as a child, and striving in his weakness to
comfort those who needed his support ; now as then he
turned to Grosvenor Bedford for a heart on which he
might lay his own heart prone, letting his sorrow have its
way. " Nothing that has assailed my character, or affected
my worldly fortune, ever gave me an hour's vexation,
or deprived me of an hour's rest. My happiness has been
in my family, and there only was I vulnerable ; that
family is now divided between earth and heaven, and I
must pray to remain with those who are left, so long as I
can contribute to their welfare and comfort, rather than
be gathered (as otherwise I would fain be) to those who
are gone." On that day of which the word Τετέλεσται is
the record, the day on which the body of his bright Isabel
was committed to earth, Southey wrote a letter to his three
living daughters, copied with his own hand for each. It
said what he could not bear to say of consolation and

N

admonishment by word of mouth; it prepared them
for the inevitable partings to come; it urged on them
with tender solicitude the duty of self-watchfulness, of
guarding against little faults, of bearing and forbearing;
it told them of his own grief to think that he should ever
by a harsh or hasty word have given their dead sister even
a momentary sorrow which might have been spared; it
ended with the blessing of their afflicted father.

Sorrows of this kind, as Southey has truly said, come
the heavier when they are repeated; under such strokes
a courageous heart may turn coward. On Mrs. Southey
a weight as of years had been laid; her spirits sank, her
firmness gave way, a breath of danger shook her. Southey's
way of bearing himself towards the dead is that saddest
way—their names were never uttered; each one of the
household had, as it were, a separate chamber in which the
images of their dead ones lay, and each went in alone and
veiled. The truth is, Southey had little native hardihood
of temperament; self-control with him was painfully acquired. In solitude and darkness his tears flowed; when
in his slumbers the images of the dead came to him, he
could not choose but weep. Therefore all the more among
those whom he wished to lead into the cheerful ways of
life, he had need to keep a guard upon his tenderness. He
feared to preserve relics, and did not like to bear in mind
birthdays, lest they should afterwards become too dangerously charged with remembrance and grief. "Look," he
writes, "at some verses in the Literary Souvenir, p. 113;
they are written by a dear friend of mine on the death of
—you will know who"—for his pen would have trembled
in tracing the name Isabel. And yet his habitual feelings with respect to those who had departed were not
bitter; the dead were absent—that was all; he thought

of them and of living friends at a distance with the same
complacency, the same affection, only with more tenderness of the dead.

Greta Hall, once resounding with cheerful voices, had
been growing silent.   Herbert was gone, Isabel was gone.
In 1829 Sara Coleridge went a bride tearful, yet glad,
her mother accompanying her, to distant London.   Five
years later Edith May Southey became the wife of the
Rev. John Warter.   Her father fell back even more than
in former years, upon the never-failing friends of his
library.   It was in these darkening years that he sought
relief in carrying out the idea, conceived long before, of a
story which should be no story, but a spacious receptacle
for mingled wit and wisdom, experience and book-lore,
wholesome nonsense and solemn meditation.   *The Doctor*
begun in jest after merry talks with Grosvenor Bedford,
grew more and more earnest as Southey proceeded.   " He
dreamt over it and brooded over it, laid it aside for months
and years, resumed it after long intervals, and more often
latterly in thoughtfulness than in mirth, and fancied at
last that he could put into it more of his mind than could
conveniently be produced in any other form."   The secret
of its authorship was carefully kept.   Southey amused
himself somewhat laboriously with ascribing it now to
this hand and now to that.   When the first two volumes
arrived, as if from the anonymous author, Southey thrust
them away with well assumed impatience, and the disdainful words, "Some novel I suppose."   Yet several
of his friends had shrewd suspicions that the manuscript
lay somewhere hidden in Greta Hall, and on receiving
their copies wrote to thank the veritable donor; these
thanks were forwarded by Southey, not without a smile
in which something of irony mingled, to Theodore Hook,

who was not pleased to enter into the jest. " I see in
The Doctor," says its author, playing the part of an
impartial critic, " a little of Rabelais, but not much ; more
of Tristram Shandy, somewhat of Burton, and perhaps
more of Montaigne ; but methinks the *quintum quid*
predominates ? " The *quintum quid* is that wisdom of the
heart, that temper of loyal and cheerful acquiescence in
the rule of life as appointed by a Divine Master, which
characterizes Southey.

For the third volume of *The ·Doctor* in that chapter
which tells of Leonard Bacon's sorrow for his Margaret,
Southey wrote as follows :

Leonard had looked for consolation, where, when sincerely
sought, it is always to be found ; and he had experienced that
religion effects in a true believer all that philosophy professes,
and more than all that mere philosophy can perform. The
wounds which stoicism would cauterize, religion heals.

There is a resignation with which, it may be feared, most of
us deceive ourselves. To bear what must be borne, and submit
to what cannot be resisted, is no more than what the unre-
generate heart is taught by the instinct of animal nature. But
to acquiesce in the afflictive dispensations of Providence—to
make one's own will conform in all things to that of our
Heavenly Father, to say to him in the sincerity of faith, when
we drink of the bitter cup, " Thy will be done ! "—to bless the
name of the Lord as much from the heart when he takes away,
as when he gives, and with a depth of feeling, of which, perhaps,
none but the afflicted heart is capable,—this is the resignation
which religion teaches, this is the sacrifice which it requires.

These words written with no forefeeling, were the last
put on paper before the great calamity burst upon Southey.
" I have been parted from my wife," he tells Grosvenor
Bedford on October 2, 1834, " by something worse than
death. Forty years she has been the life of my life ; and
I have left her this day in a lunatic asylum."

Southey's union with his wife had been at the first one
of love, and use and wont had made her a portion of
his very being.   Their provinces in the household had
soon defined themselves.   He in the library earned their
means of support; all else might be left to her with
absolute confidence in her wise contrivance and quiet
energy.   Beneath the divided work in their respective
provinces their lives ran on in deep and still accord.
Now he felt for the first time shrunk into the limits of a
solitary will.   All that had grown out of the past was
deranged by a central disturbance; no branch had been
lopped away, but the main trunk was struck, and seared,
and shaken to the roots.   "Mine is a strong heart;"
Southey writes, "I will not say that the last week has been
the most trying of my life; but I will say, that the heart
which could bear it can bear anything."   Yet when he
once more set himself to work, a common observer, says
his son, would have noticed little change in him, though
to his family the change was great indeed.   His most
wretched hour was when he woke at dawn from broken
slumbers; but a word of hope was enough to coun-
teract the mischief of a night's unrest.   No means were
neglected which might serve to keep him in mental and
bodily health; he walked in all weathers; he pursued
his task-work diligently, yet not over-diligently; he
collected materials for work of his choice.   When in
the spring of 1835 it was found that the sufferer might
return to wear out the body of this death in her own
home, it was marvellous, declares Cuthbert Southey, how
much of his old elasticity remained, and how though
no longer happy, he could be contented and cheerful, and
take pleasure in the pleasures of others.   He still could
contribute something to his wife's comfort.   Through the

weary dream which was now her life she knew him, and
took pleasure in his coming and going.

When Herbert died, Southey had to ask a friend to lend
him money to tide over the short period of want which
followed his weeks of enforced inaction. Happily now
for the first time in his life his income was beforehand
with his expenses. A bequest of some hundreds of
pounds had come in; his *Naval Biographies* were paying
him well, and during part of Mrs. Southey's illness he
was earning a respectable sum, intended for his son's
education, by his *Life of Cowper*, a work to which a
painful interest was added by the study of mental aliena-
tion forced upon him in his own household. So the days
passed not altogether cheerlessly, in work if possible
more arduous than ever. "One morning," writes his
son, "shortly after the letters had arrived, he called
me into his study. 'You will be surprised,' he said, 'to
hear that Sir Robert Peel has recommended me to the
King for the distinction of a baronetcy, and will probably
feel some disappointment when I tell you that I shall not
accept it.'" Accompanying Sir Robert Peel's official com-
munication came a private letter asking in the kindest
manner how he could be of use to Southey. "Will
you tell me," he said, "without reserve, whether the
possession of power puts within my reach the means of
doing anything which can be serviceable or acceptable
to you; and whether you will allow me to find some
compensation for the many sacrifices which office imposes
upon me, in the opportunity of marking my gratitude as a
public man, for the eminent services you have rendered,
not only to literature, but to the higher interests of virtue
and religion?" Southey's answer stated simply what his
circumstances were, showing how unbecoming and unwise

it would be to accept the proffered honour; it told
the friendly statesman of the provision made for his
family—no inconsiderable one—in the event of his death;
it went on to speak of his recent affliction; how this had
sapped his former confidence in himself; how it had
made him an old man and forced upon him the reflection that a sudden stroke might deprive him of those
faculties, by which his family had hitherto been supported.
"I could afford to die, but not to be disabled," he wrote in
his first draft, but fearing that these words would look as
if he wanted to trick out pathetically a plain statement,
he removed them.   Finally, if such an increase of his
pension as would relieve him from anxiety on behalf of
his family could form part of a plan for the encouragement
of literature, it would satisfy all his desires.   " Young as I
then was," Cuthbert Southey writes, " I could not, without
tears, hear him read with his deep and faltering voice, his
wise refusal and touching expression of those feelings and
fears he had never before given utterance to, to any of
his own family."   Two months later Sir Robert Peel
signed a warrant adding 300*l.* annually to Southey's existing pension.   He had resolved to recognize literary and
scientific eminence as a national claim; the act was done
upon public grounds, and Southey had the happiness of
knowing that others beside himself would partake of the
benefit.

" Our domestic prospects are darkening upon us daily,"
Southey wrote in July, 1835.   " I know not whether the
past or the present seems most like a dream to me, so great
and strange is the difference.   But, yet a little while, and
all will again be at the best."   While Mrs. Southey
lived, a daily demand was made upon his sympathies and
solicitude which it was his happiness to fulfil.   But

from all except his wife he seemed already to be drop-
ping away into a state of passive abstraction.   Kate and
Bertha silently ministered to his wants, laid the books he
wanted in his way, replenished his ink-bottle, mended
his pens, stirred the fire, and said nothing.   A visit to
the south-west of England in company with his son broke
the long monotony of endurance.   It was a happiness to
meet Landor at Bristol, and Mrs. Bray at Tavistock,
and Mrs. Bray's friend, the humble poet, Mary Colling,
whose verses he had reviewed in the *Quarterly*.   Yet to
return to his sorrowful home was best of all; there is a
leap up of the old spirits in a letter to his daughters an-
nouncing his approach.   It is almost the last gleam of brightness.   In the autumn of that year (1837) Edith Southey
wasted away, growing weaker and weaker.   The strong
arm on which she had leaned for two and forty years
supported her down stairs each day and bore her up
again at evening.   When the morning of November 16th
broke, she passed quietly "from death unto life."

From that day Southey was an altered man.   His
spirits fell to a still lower range.   For the first time he
was conscious of the distance which years had set between
him and his children.   Yet his physical strength was
unbroken; nothing but snow deterred him from his
walk; he could still circle the lake, or penetrate
into Borrowdale on foot.   But Echo, whom he had summoned to rejoice, was not roused by any call of his.
Within doors it was only by a certain violence to
himself that he could speak.   In the library he read
aloud his proof sheets alone; but for this he might
almost have forgotten the sound of his own voice.   Still
he was not wholly abandoned to grief; he looked back
and saw that life had been good; its hardest moral dis-

cipline had served to train the heart: much still remained that was of worth; Cuthbert was quietly pursuing
his Oxford studies; Bertha was about to be united in
marriage to her cousin Herbert Hill, son of that good
uncle who had done so much to shape Southey's career.
" If not hopeful," he writes, " I am more than contented, and disposed to welcome and entertain any
good that may yet be in store for me, without any
danger of being disappointed if there should be none."
Hope of a sober kind indeed had come to him. For
twenty years he had known Caroline Bowles; they
had long been in constant correspondence; their acquaintance had matured into friendship. She was now in
her fifty-second year; he, in his sixty-fifth. It seemed
to Southey natural that without making any breach with
his past life, he should accept her companionship in the
nearest way possible, should give to her all he could of
what remained, and save himself from that forlorn feeling
which he feared might render old age miserable and
useless.

But already the past had subdued Southey, and if any
future lay before him it was a cloud lifeless and grey. In
the autumn of 1838 he started for a short tour on the
Continent with his old friend Senhouse, his son Cuthbert,
John Kenyon, their master of the horse, Captain Jones, the
chamberlain, and Crabb Robinson, who was intendant and
paid the bills. On the way from Boulogne they turned
aside to visit Chinon, for Southey wished to stand on the
spot where his first heroine, Joan of Arc, had recognized the
French king. At Paris he roamed along the quays and
hunted bookstalls. The change and excitement seemed to
have served him; he talked freely and was cheerful. "Still,"
writes his son, " I could not fail to perceive a considerable

change in him from the time we had last travelled together
—all his movements were slower, he was subject to frequent
fits of absence, and there was an indecision in his manner
and an unsteadiness in his step which was wholly unusual with him." He often lost his way, even in the
hotels; then laughed at his own mistakes, and yet was
painfully conscious of his failing memory. His journal
breaks off abruptly when not more than two-thirds of the
tour had been accomplished. In February, 1839, his
brother, Dr. Southey—ever a true comrade—describes him
as working slowly and with an abstraction not usual to
him; sometimes to write even a letter seemed an effort.
In midsummer his marriage to Caroline Bowles took
place, and with her he returned to Keswick in August.
On the way home his friends in London saw that
he was much altered. "The animation and peculiar
clearness of his mind," wrote Henry Taylor, "was quite
gone, except a gleam or two now and then. . . . . The
appearance was that of a placid languor, sometimes approaching to torpor, but not otherwise than cheerful. He
is thin and shrunk in person, and that extraordinary face
of his has no longer the fire and strength it used to have,
though the singular cast of the features and the habitual
expressions make it still a most remarkable phenomenon."
Still his friends had not ceased to hope that tranquillity
would restore mental tone, and he himself was planning
the completion of great designs. "As soon as we are
settled at Keswick, I shall resolutely begin upon the *History of Portugal*, as a duty which I owe to my uncle's
memory. Half of the labour I consider as done. But I
have long since found the advantage of doing more than
one thing at a time, and the *History of the Monastic Orders*
is the other thing to which I shall set to with hearty

good will.   Both these are works of great pith and moment."

Alas, the current of these enterprises was already turned awry. In August it was not without an occasional uncertainty that he sustained conversation. "He lost himself for a moment; he was conscious of it, and an expression passed over his countenance which was very touching—an expression of pain and also of resignation. . . . . The charm of his manner is perhaps even enhanced at present (at least when one knows the circumstances) by the gentleness and patience which pervade it." Before long the character of his handwriting, which had been so exquisite, was changed to something like the laboured scrawl of a child; then he ceased to write. Still he could read, and, even when he could no longer take in the meaning of what was before him, his eye followed the lines of the printed page. At last even this was beyond his power. He would walk slowly round his library, pleased with the presence of his cherished possessions, taking some volume down mechanically from the shelf. In 1840 Wordsworth went over to Greta Hall. " Southey did not recognize me," he writes, " till he was told. Then his eyes flashed for a moment with their former brightness, but he sank into the state in which I had found him, patting with both hands his books affectionately like a child." In the *Life of Cowper* he had spoken of the distress of one who suffers from mental disease as being that of a dream, " a dream indeed from which the sufferer can neither wake nor be awakened; but it pierces no deeper, and there seems to be the same dim consciousness of its unreality." So was it now with himself. Until near the end he retained considerable bodily strength; his snow-white hair grew darker; it was the spirit which had endured shattering strokes of fate, and which had spent itself in studying to be quiet.

After a short attack of fever, the end came on the 21st of March, 1843. Never was that " Well done," the guerdon of the good and faithful servant, pronounced amid a deeper consent of those who attended and had ears to hear. On a dark and stormy morning Southey's body was borne to the beautiful churchyard of Crosthwaite, towards which he had long looked affectionately as his place of rest. There lay his three children and she who was the life of his life. Skiddaw gloomed solemnly overhead. A grey-haired, venerable man who had crossed the hills stood there leaning on the arm of his son-in-law ; these two, Wordsworth and Quillinan, were the only strangers present. As the words, " ashes to ashes," were uttered, a sudden gleam of sunshine touched the grave ; the wind dropped, the rain was over, and the birds had begun their songs of spring. The mourners turned away thinking of a good man's life and death with peace—

And calm of mind, all passion spent

CHAPTER VII.

SOUTHEY'S career of authorship falls into two chief periods —a period during which poetry occupied the higher place and prose the lower, and a period during which this order was reversed. His translations of romantic fiction—*Amadis of Gaul, Palmerin of England,* and *The Cid*—connect the work of the earlier with that of the latter period, and serve to mark the progress of his mind from legend to history and from the fantastic to the real. The poet in Southey died young, or, if he did not die, fell into a numbness and old age like that of which an earlier singer writes :—

> Elde that in my spirit dulleth me,
> Hath of endyting all the subtilité
> Welnyghe bereft out of my remembraunce.

After thirty Southey seldom cared to utter himself in occasional verse. The uniformity of his life, the equable cheerfulness maintained by habits of regular work, his calm religious faith, his amiable Stoicism left him without the material for lyrical poetry ; and one so honest and healthy had no care to feign experiences of the heart which were not his. Still he could apply himself to the treatment of large subjects with a calm continuous energy ; but as time went on his hand grew slack, and wrought with less ease. Scarcely had he overcome the narrative poet's chief difficulty, that of subduing varied materials to an unity of design, when he put aside verse and found it more natural to be historian than poet.

The poetry of sober feeling is rare in lyrical verse. This may be found admirably rendered in some of Southey's shorter pieces. Although his temper was ardent and hopeful, his poems of pensive remembrance, of meditative calm, are perhaps the most characteristic. Among these his *Inscriptions* rank high. Some of those in memory of the dead are remarkable for their fine poise of feeling, all that is excessive and transitory having been subdued; for the tranquil depths of sorrow and of hope which lie beneath their clear, melodious words.

Southey's larger poetical works are fashioned of two materials, which do not always entirely harmonize. First, material brought from his own moral nature; his admiration of something elevated in the character of man or woman —generosity, gentleness, loyalty, fortitude, faith. And secondly, material gathered from abroad ; mediæval pomps of religion and circumstance of war; Arabian marvels, the work of the enchanters and the genii ; the wild beauties and adventure of life amid New-world tribes; the monstrous mythology of the Brahman. With such material the poet's inventive talent deals freely, rearranges details or adds to them ; still Southey is here rather a *finder* than a *maker*. His diligence in collecting and his skill in arranging were so great that it was well if the central theme did not disappear among manifold accessories. One who knows Southey, however, can recognize his ethical spirit in every poem. Thalaba, as he himself confessed, is a male Joan of Arc. Destiny or Providence has marked alike the hero and the heroine from mankind ; the sheep-

fold of Domremi, and the palm-grove by old Moath's tent,
alike nurture virgin purity and lofty aspiration. Thalaba,
like Joan, goes forth a delegated servant of the Highest
to war against the powers of evil; Thalaba, like Joan, is
sustained under the trials of the way by the sole talisman
of faith. We are not left in doubt as to where Southey
found his ideal. Mr. Barbauld thought Joan of Arc was
modelled on the Socinian Christ. He was mistaken;
Southey's ideal was native to his soul. " Early admiration, almost adoration of Leonidas, early principles of
Stoicism derived from the habitual study of Epictetus,
and the French Revolution at its height when I was just
eighteen—by these my mind was moulded." And from
these, absorbed into Southey's very being, came Thalaba
and Joan.

The word *high-souled* takes possession of the mind as we
think of Southey's heroic personages. Poetry, he held,
ought rather to elevate than to affect—a Stoical doctrine
transferred to art, which meant that his own poetry was
derived more from admiration of great qualities, than from
sympathy with individual men or women. Neither the
quick and passionate tenderness of Burns, nor the stringent
pathos of Wordsworth, can be found in Southey's verse.
No eye probably ever shed a tear over the misery of Ladurlad and his persecuted daughter. She, like the lady
in *Comus*, is set above our pity and perhaps our love. In
Kehama, a work of Southey's mature years, the chivalric
ardour of his earlier heroes is transformed into the sterner
virtues of fortitude and an almost despairing constancy.
The power of evil, as conceived by the poet, has grown
more despotic; little can be achieved by the light-winged
Glendoveer—a more radiant Thalaba—against the Rajah;
only the lidless eye of Seeva can destroy that tyranny of

lust and pride. *Roderick* marks a higher stage in the development of Southey's ethical ideal. Roderick too is a delegated champion of right against force and fraud ; he too endures mighty pains. But he is neither such a combatant, pure and intrepid, as goes forth from the Arab tent, nor such a blameless martyr as Ladurlad. He is first a sinner enduring just punishment ; then a stricken penitent ; and from his shame and remorse he is at last uplifted by enthusiasm on behalf of his God and his people into a warrior saint, the Gothic Maccabee.

Madoc stands somewhat away from the line of Southey's other narrative poems. Though, as Scott objected, the personages in *Madoc* are too nearly abstract types, Southey's ethical spirit dominates this poem less than any of the others. The narrative flows on more simply. The New-world portion tells a story full of picturesque incident, with the same skill and grace that belong to Southey's best prose writings. Landor highly esteemed *Madoc*. Scott declared that he had read it three times since his first cursory perusal, and each time with increased admiration of the poetry. Fox was in the habit of reading aloud after supper to eleven o'clock, when it was the rule at St. Ann's Hill to retire ; but while *Madoc* was in his hand, he read until after midnight. Those, however, who opened the bulky quarto were few ; the tale was out of relation with the time ; it interpreted no need, no aspiration, no passion of the dawn of the present century. And the mind of the time was not enough disengaged to concern itself deeply with the supposed adventures of a Welsh prince of the twelfth century among the natives of America.

At heart, then, Southey's poems are in the main the outcome of his moral nature ; this we recognize through all

disguises, Mohammedan, Hindoo, or Catholic. He planned
and partly wrote a poem—*Oliver Newman*—which should
associate his characteristic ideal with Puritan principles
and ways of life. The foreign material through which his
ethical idea was set forth went far, with each poem, to
determine its reception by the public. Coleridge has
spoken of "the pastoral charm and wild streaming lights
of the *Thalaba*." Dewy night moon-mellowed, and the
desert-circle girdled by the sky, the mystic palace of
Shedad, the vernal brook, Oneiza's favourite kidling, the
lamp-light shining rosy through the damsel's delicate
fingers, the aged Arab in the tent-door,—these came with
a fresh charm into English narrative poetry eighty years
ago. The landscape and the manners of Spain, as pictured in *Roderick*, are of marked grandeur and simplicity.
In *Kehama* Southey attempted a bolder experiment, and
although the poem became popular, even a well-disposed
reader may be allowed to sympathize with the dismay of
Charles Lamb among the monstrous gods : " I never read
books of travels, at least not farther than Paris or Rome.
I can just endure Moors, because of their connexion as
foes with Christians ; but Abyssinians, Ethiops, Esqui-
maux, Dervises, and all that tribe I hate. I believe I
fear them in some manner. A Mohammedan turban on
the stage, though enveloping some well-known face, ...
does not give me unalloyed pleasure. I am a Christian,
Englishman, Londoner, Templar. God help me when I
come to put off these snug relations, and to get abroad into
the world to come."

Though his materials are often exotic, in style Southey
aimed at the simplicity and strength of undefiled English.
If to these melody was added, he had attained all he desired. To conversations with William Taylor about Ger-

o

man poetry—certainly not to Taylor's example—he ascribes his faith in the power of plain words to express in poetry the highest thoughts and strongest feelings. He perceived in his own day the rise of the ornate style, which has since been perfected by Tennyson, and he regarded it as a vice in art. In early years Akenside had been his instructor ; afterwards he owed more to Landor than to any other master of style. From *Madoc* and *Roderick*—both in blank verse—fragments could be severed, which might pass for the work of Landor ; but Southey's free and facile manner, fostered by early reading of Ariosto, and by constant study of Spenser, soon reasserts itself ; from under the fragment of monumental marble, white almost as Landor's, a stream wells out smooth and clear, and lapses away never dangerously swift nor mysteriously deep. On the whole, judged by the highest standards, Southey's poetry takes a midmost rank ; it neither renders into art a great body of thought and passion, nor does it give faultless expression to lyrical moments. But it is the out-put of a large and vigorous mind, amply stored with knowledge ; its breath of life is the moral ardour of a nature strong and generous, and therefore it can never cease to be of worth.

Southey is at his best in prose. And here it must be borne in mind that, though so voluminous a writer, he did not achieve his most important work, the *History of Portugal*, for which he had gathered vast collections. It cannot be doubted that this, if completed, would have taken a place among our chief histories. The splendour of story and the heroic personages would have lifted Southey into his highest mood. We cannot speak with equal confidence of his projected work of second magnitude, the *History of the Monastic Orders*. Learned and sensible it could not

fail to be, and Southey would have recognized the more
substantial services of the founders and the brotherhoods ;
but he would have dealt by methods too simple with the
psychology of religious emotions ; the words enthusiasm
and fraud might have risen too often to his lips ; and at
the grotesque humours of the devout, which he would have
exhibited with delight, he might have been too prone to
smile.

As it is, Southey's largest works are not his most admirable. *The History of Brazil,* indeed, gives evidence
of amazing patience, industry, and skill ; but its subject
necessarily excludes it from the first rank. At no time
from the sixteenth to the nineteenth century was Brazil
a leader or a banner-bearer among lands. The life of the
people crept on from point to point, and that is all ; there
are few passages in which the chronicle can gather itself
up, and transform itself into a historic drama. Southey
has done all that was possible ; his pages are rich in facts,
and are more entertaining than perhaps any other writer
could have made them. His extraordinary acquaintance
with travel gave him many advantages in narrating the
adventures of early explorers ; and his studies in ecclesiastical history led him to treat with peculiar interest the
history of the Jesuit Reductions.

The History of the Peninsular War suffers by com-
parison with the great work of Sir William Napier. That
heroic man had himself been a portion of the strife ; his
senses singularly keen were attuned to battle ; as he wrote,
the wild bugle-calls, the measured tramp, the peals of
musketry, the dismal clamour sounded in his ears ; he
abandoned himself again to the swiftness and " incredible
fury " of the charge. And with his falcon eye he could
discern amid the shock or formless dispersion, wherever

hidden, the fiery heart of victory.   Southey wrought in
his library as a man of letters ; consulted sources, turned
over manuscripts, corresponded with witnesses, set his
material in order.   The passion of justice and an enthusiasm on behalf of Spain give unity to his work.   If he
estimated too highly the disinterestedness and courage of
the people of the Peninsula, the illusion was generous.
And it may be that enduring spiritual forces become
apparent to a distant observer, which are masked by
accidents of the day and hour from one who is in their
midst.

History as written by Southey is narrative rendered
spiritual by moral ardour.   There are no new political
truths, he said.   If there be laws of a nation's life other
than those connected with elementary principles of morality, Southey did not discover these.   What he has
written may go only a little way towards attaining the
ultimate ends of historical study, but so far as it goes it
keeps the direct line.   It is not led astray by will-o'-the-
wisp, vague-shining theories that beguile night wanderers.
Its method is an honest method as wholesome as sweet ;
and simple narrative if ripe and sound at first is none the
less so at the end of a century.

In biography, at least, one may be well pleased with
clear and charming narrative.   Here Southey has not been
surpassed, and even in this single province he is versatile ;
he has written the life of a warrior, of a poet, and of a
saint.   His industry was that of a German ; his lucidity
and perfect exposition were such as we rarely find outside
a French memoir.   There is no style fitter for continuous
narrative than the pedestrian style of Southey.   It does
not beat upon the ear with hard metallic vibration.   The
sentences are not cast by the thousand in one mould of

cheap rhetoric, nor made brilliant with one cheap colour. Never dithyrambic, he is never dull ; he affects neither the trick of stateliness nor that of careless ease ; he does not seek out curiosities of refinement, nor caress delicate affectations. Because his style is natural it is inimitable, and the only way to write like Southey is to write well.

"The favourite of my library, among many favourites;" so Coleridge speaks of the *Life of Wesley*, "the book I can read for the twentieth time, when I can read nothing else at all." And yet the school-boy's favourite, the *Life of Nelson*, is of happier inspiration. The simple and chivalric hero, his splendid achievements, his pride in duty, his patriotism, roused in Southey all that was most strong and high ; but his enthusiasm does not escape in lyrical speech. "The best eulogy of Nelson," he says, "is the faithful history of his actions ; the best history that which shall relate them most perspicuously." Only when all is over, and the captain of Trafalgar lies dead, his passion and pride find utterance :—"If the chariot and the horses of fire had been vouchsafed for Nelson's translation, he could scarcely have departed in a brighter blaze of glory." From Nelson on the quarter-deck of the *Victory*, to Cowper caressing his tame hares, the interval is wide ; but Southey, the man of letters, lover of the fireside, and patron of cats, found it natural to sympathize with his brother poet. His sketches of literary history in the *Life of Cowper* are characteristic. The writer's range is wide, his judgment sound, his enjoyment of almost everything literary is lively ; as critic he is kindly yet equitable. But the highest criticism is not his. Southey's vision was not sufficiently penetrative ; he culls beauties, but he cannot pluck out the heart of a mystery.

His translations of romantic fiction, while faithful to

their sources, aim less at literal exactitude than at giving
the English reader the same pleasure which the Spaniard
receives from the originals. From the destruction of Don
Quixote's library Master Nicholas and the curate spared
Amadis of Gaul and *Palmerin of England*. Second to
Malory's grouping of the Arthur cycle *Amadis* may well
take its place. Its chivalric spirit, its wildness, its tenderness and beauty are carefully preserved by the translator.
But Southey's chief gift in this kind to English readers is
The Cid. The poem he supposed, indeed, to be a metrical
chronicle instead of a metrical romance—no fatal error ;
weaving together the best of the poem, the ballads and the
chronicle, he produced more than a mere compilation. " I
know no work of the kind in our language," wrote Coleridge, " none which, uniting the charms of romance and
history, keeps the imagination so constantly on the wing,
and yet leaves so much for after reflection."

Of Southey's political writings something has been said
in a former chapter. Among works which can be brought
under no general head, one that pleased the public was
Espriella's Letters, sketches of English landscape, life, and
manners, by a supposed Spanish traveller. The letters,
giving as they do a lively view of England at the beginning of the present century, still possess an interest. Apart
from Southey's other works stands *The Doctor ;* nowhere
else can one find so much of his varied erudition, his genial
spirits, his meditative wisdom. It asks for a leisurely
reader content to ramble everywhere and no whither, and
still pleased to take another turn because his companion
has not yet come to an end of learning, mirth, or meditation. That the author of a book so characteristic was not
instantly recognized is strange. " The wit and humour
of *The Doctor*," says Edgar Poe, a keen critic, " have sel-

dom been equalled.   We cannot think Southey wrote it."
Gratitude is due to Doctor Daniel Dove from innumerable
" good little women and men," who have been delighted
with his story of *The Three Bears*.   To know that he had
added a classic to the nursery would have been the pride
of Southey's heart.   Wide eyes entranced and peals of
young laughter still make a triumph for one whose spirit,
grave with a man's wisdom, was pure as the spirit of a
little child.

THE END.